Introduction to
SAILING

Introduction to
to

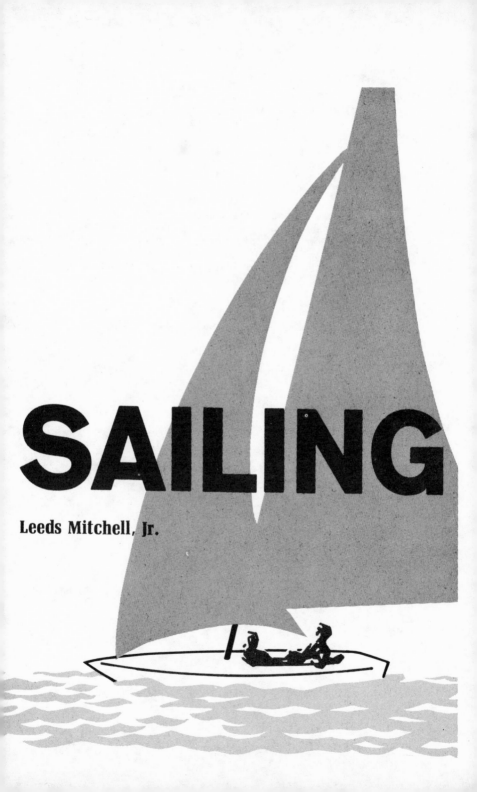

SAILING

Leeds Mitchell, Jr.

INTRODUCTION TO SAILING
Copyright © 1971 by
THE STACKPOLE COMPANY

Published by
STACKPOLE BOOKS
Cameron and Kelker Streets
Harrisburg, Pa. 17105

This is a RUBICON BOOK, 1974 edition, of the hardbound book originally published in 1971.

With many drawings by and based on the work of
Margery D. Mitchell.

ISBN: 0-8117-2032-2 (pap.)

Price: $2.95
Printed in U.S.A.

CONTENTS

Foreword

This book is a sailing primer, written for the novice—more specifically the adult novice. Its text is tailored to the learning process in boats within the 14 to 24-foot range. It emphasizes *the importance of starting out in light winds only.*

There is no substitute for personal instruction, however, this book may be used in conjunction with such instruction. For those who cannot find such instruction, the book will serve as a complete text to provide a safe entree into an absorbing and fascinating sport.

It is suggested that the material be absorbed prior to one's first sail, referred to during and after each sail, and retained as a reference during the winter and other times when sailing is not pleasant. Anyone who does absorb the material and who keeps clearly in mind the limitations—light airs, small to medium-sized boats—will quickly gain the confidence needed to go further into the challenging complications of advanced aspects of the sport, and will then be ready for the myriad books available for this end of the learning curve.

L. M. Jr.

chapter 1

The Adventure of Sailing

Few sports can match the challenge of sailing. From the intrepid navigator who single-handedly sails his 55-foot ketch around the world to the weekend voyager who takes his boat out in only the lightest of winds and never ventures more than a few hundred yards from shore, sailors pit themselves against the elements with a minimum of mechanical advantage.

Countless people with sedentary jobs would rather be out under nature's canopy coping with elemental instead of artificial problems. Why else would they ski, fly, hike, climb mountains, or sail? Psychologists say that human beings need a certain dash of challenge and danger in their lives in order to handle their vocational tasks with optimum efficiency.

Sailing offers this needed challenge to beginners and veterans alike. In fact, the more one knows about sailing, the more exciting it becomes. Learning the needed nautical skills—seamanship, navigation, ship's husbandry, judgment, coordination of mind and muscle, knowledge of wind and tide—provides the satisfaction that comes with mastery; but no matter how much one knows, there is always more to learn.

Not only does sailing supply the kind of challenge missing in the ordinary workaday world, it offers a serenity that is hard to come by in the congested urban areas where so many people work. Most sailable waterways are incomparably more quiet, cleaner, and less crowded than most city roads and country highways. True, there are boatmen with the same lack of manners their counterparts exhibit ashore, but there is a greater expanse of space in which to elude the inconsiderate.

Best of all, sailing is for everyone—the well-to-do and those of modest means, men and women, young and old. Back in the 1920s, a yacht was synonymous with wealth. However, in industrialized countries since World War II, more widespread affluence and boat builders' utilization of new materials and techniques have brought boat prices within reach of a vast new public. Today anyone who can afford a sport can afford sailing.

Strength is no more needed to enjoy sailing than is money. In sailboats under thirty-five feet in length only few tasks require real strength, and these can be handled by learning tricks of leverage. Any woman who is interested can learn to do anything there is to do on a sailboat as quickly and as easily as any man. No wonder more and more women are enrolling in sailing schools. When they graduate, they are well able to keep up with their husbands in the sport.

Sailing is for the youngsters as well as the ladies. Yacht clubs have sailing classes for young people of almost any age, provided that the applicants furnish proof of their ability to swim. Colleges and some high schools have sailing teams, many of which participate in national intercollegiate competition. Almost all of these young people will stay with the sport for life.

At present, the largest segment of the sailboat-buying public consists of people between the ages of twenty-five and forty, latecomers along with confirmed "second genera-tion" old-timers. Sailors of more advanced years are mostly old-timers, but a sprinkling of newcomers is joining their ranks. As the broad interest in sailing continues, it seems likely that its devotees will be drawn almost equally from all age groups and that it will become even more of a family activity, promoting the best kind of togetherness.

chapter 2

Getting
Started

The speed with which people learn sailing skills largely depends upon mental attitudes. Perhaps the most important asset to learning is enthusiasm, a factor which varies widely among individuals. Anxiety constitutes the most powerful hindrance to acquiring boat-handling skills.

Women and youngsters have advantages in overcoming anxiety about boats and water. In our society, women can admit such fear more readily than men; and, of course, it is easier to deal with feelings of insecurity when they are out in the open. Youngsters have not had the time to acquire the anxieties accumulated by adults.

A reasonably coordinated youngster eight to ten years of age can teach himself to sail simply by doing it, although he should not try to learn this way if the practice area has anchored boats or moving traffic. However, he will learn much more quickly and with far fewer bad habits if he is helped by experienced sailors. The better yacht clubs have excellent programs of instruction for young people.

Because yacht clubs seldom offer classes for adults, grown-ups usually must go to one of the few sailing schools for formal instruction, although the Power Squadrons and Coast Guard auxiliaries offer excellent winter courses. Most yacht brokers and stores which deal in sailing items have published lists of sailing schools throughout the United States, almost all on the east and west coasts. Some of these schools cater to all ages, some to youngsters or adults only. Some specialize in navigation, some in fundamentals, others in a wide range of skills.

Lacking a yacht club or a school, the beginning sailor may ask a knowledgeable friend for instruction. If the friend is not truly knowledgeable, however, the student will probably pick up bad habits. Moreover, most sailors will not let anyone near the steering mechanism of their boats and their pupils will likely spend most of their time obeying orders blindly.

The beginning sailor without access to formal instruction or a rare boating friend must rely on reading and practicing in combination. A great many people are learning to sail by reading books and buying boats in which to practice their reading-learning. Remember, though, that either reading or practicing alone will yield slower and more questionable results.

In selecting a book, make sure that it is written simply and puts first things first. It should not mix advanced insights with basics. Illustrations are especially important, for many readers learn more easily from drawings than from prose. Diagrams should be both simple and inclusive enough to be readily intelligible.

Whether learning from a teacher or by book, the beginner in sailing must contend with a wealth of jargon found in no other sport. The reader of this book, however, need not distract himself at the outset by learning a new language. Most terms used herein are everyday English. Of course, in time, every sailor should master the nautical nomenclature, and a glossary in the back of the book will help him do so.

As with most skills worth acquiring, sailing skill comes in fits and starts. The first lesson or practice session usually discourages. The second usually gives one a rather euphoric sense of major accomplishment which is jarringly run aground the third time out, when nothing can be done correctly.

After four or five lessons or practice excursions the average student will be able to take a boat out in friendly weather, sail it around, and get it back to mooring and put to bed. Thereafter, the art of sailing (for such it is) will be seen as a vista stretching far past the horizon.

chapter 3

Picking the Right Boat

Sailboats come in sizes, shapes, and styles to please every taste. An individual should purchase the boat which best suits his personal needs.

Beginners often wonder whether it is unwise to purchase a boat before they have enough experience to know the full range of variety available and the advantages of each type. They need not worry; old-timers change boats often. Provided that a newcomer to sailing learns enough to avoid buying a boat in irremediably poor condition, or inferior design, or of a type unsuited to the area in which it will be sailed, he can buy a boat even before he learns to sail. Free or low-cost advice available in all sailing areas will enable the beginner to skirt these pitfalls. Unfortunately, few harbors have facilities which charter (rent) sailboats, and selection is restricted.

Keels vs. Centerboards

Every sailboat must have some sort of fin under it to keep from crabbing sidewise when the wind comes from the side. Such a fin provides most of what the sailor calls "lateral plane." Lateral plane can be attained from a keel (fixed), a centerboard (movable up and down on a hinge), a dagger board (movable by manual lifting or downward inserting), or lee boards (movable, one on either side of a boat). Only small boats have dagger boards, and lee boards are for specialized craft like sailing canoes and kayaks. Hence, most people will need to know only about keels and centerboards, but even these present a broad range of choice.

Keels may be found on boats from fifteen feet up, and centerboards on boats from seven feet up. Keels provide greater stability. Being fixed, a keel can carry much weight concentrated at its very lowest point. The result is a gravity force which counteracts the tendency of all sailboats to tip when the wind blows from one side. It would be extremely difficult to capsize a keel boat.

Because of its greatest advantage, that of being retractable into its well within the boat, the centerboard lacks stabilizing weight and, consequently, a centerboard boat can tip over. However, a centerboard boat can sail into shallower water, and is more easily trailable.

Dagger boards, often categorized as centerboards, are found in boats too small to include the longer well-box required for a hinged board. Many sailing dinghies and all board boats (Sunfish, Sailfish, etc.) utilize dagger boards.

Planing vs. Displacement

All boats have displacement; i.e., their hulls displace water. However, when a light boat skims at high speed through the water with but little displacement, it is said to be planing.

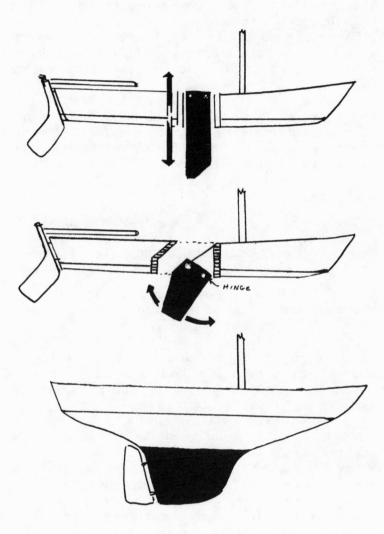

Figure 3-1. *Top:* Dagger board. *Center:* Centerboard. *Bottom:* Keel.

Since World War II, planing boats have grown remarkably in both efficiency and numbers.

For cruising and for family use, designers create displacement boats. For racing and sport, planing hulls offer the attractions of speed and quick response at the expense of space and comfort.

A displacement boat with good initial speed on the front of a wave can plane for a time, but it will quickly turn back into a displacement boat. The planing boat does not plane all the time, but it will attain a planing attitude very easily and can sustain a plane for long periods of time. A displacement boat is generally more stable than a planing one. If it isn't, it has a design fault.

Boats for Cruising,
Family Day-Sailing, or Racing

Each of these three types may be had with keel or centerboard and each comes in both planing or displacement models, within a range varying in degree.

Beginners should choose a boat in the cruising or day-sailing category. Racing is inadvisable for novices, since it requires relegating the skills of plain sailing to reflex action.

Cruising means different things to different people. To some, cruising is transoceanic navigation. To others, it is venturing ten miles to a neighboring harbor. Cruising boats have stoves, ice boxes, toilets, beds, and the comforts of a home away from home.

Any vessel meant to be used only during daylight hours presupposes the lack of the conveniences mentioned above, although some designs do include toilets, generally in cramped locations. Day-sailers come in a wide range of sizes, but most are in the 16-30 foot range, whereas most cruising boats are 22 feet or over.

Choosing a Boat to Suit Age and Personality

A youngster of twelve will not always like the same type of boat his father or grandfather does. In general, the planing centerboard boat has more attraction for the young than the keel displacement boat does. Every owner must decide whether he is still young enough for the former.

Personality is a far more important and complex factor in the decision process than age. (Of course, personality also plays a part in the decision as to one's age.) Do you want solitude or are you gregarious? Are you more readily satisfied with peace and quiet and the absence of tension, or do you need the excitement of speed and fast responses? Some sailors like to have the wife and kids along, while others need relief from them. Of course, considerations of companionship may be dictated by the needs of the boat itself; some boats can be piloted single-handedly better than others.

Buying a "Character Boat"

A "character boat" is one possessing features which do not fit well into current design patterns. Examples would be replicas of designs of a bygone era, or miniatures of functional designs. Almost always, character boats are one of a kind. To most sailors, they are simply not practical.

Beginners should beware of buying any "one of a kind" boat, such as a boat which is popular in another country or area but not in the waters in which the owner will sail. Best advice is to concentrate attention on boats which appear in large numbers in the local area. This usually presupposes boats which are raced. The fact that a boat is raced is by no means reason to look further if one wishes a cruising or day-sailing type. Many good cruising and day-sailing boats are raced very competitively, and their numbers are increasing.

Building Materials

Today boats come in a variety of materials: wood, fiberglass, steel, aluminum, and ferro-cement. Ironically, while most boat-lovers have a hankering for wood as the most romantic material, the best bargains are secondhand wooden boats. This is because wood is the most difficult to maintain. Being porous, it absorbs water and expands, or dries out and contracts, causing problems in keeping one plank against the other, and thereby admitting water. This absorbent tendency also makes it difficult to apply and sustain a finish, since even a minute amount of moisture in the grain hampers the absorption of paint or varnish. Despite all these drawbacks, wooden boats are still being built for the determined sailors who favor them.

For the person who wishes to expend a minimal amount of time in maintenance, any of the other materials offers advantages over wood. Fiberglass is the material most seen in smaller boats, and ferro-cement is just beginning to realize a potential seen by a few pioneers for many years. Only few day-sailers, small cruising boats, or racing boats are made of metal, either steel or aluminum. These materials are generally seen only in fairly large custom boats.

Of the lot, fiberglass is the most practical material. It is easy to maintain and to repair. It allows more space within a given hull size than wood, steel, or aluminum, all of which require skeletal "ribs" or "frames" on which to fasten the outside surface, or "skin." Increasingly reasonable prices of fiberglass boats have resulted from the manufacturers' ability to sell enough units to amortize the substantial costs of the original molds.

Gear and Sails

A sailboat must have high-quality hardware, the devices used for fastening ropes or for hauling them up or down, in or out, or for attaining mechanical advantage with which to do this pulling and hauling. Such devices must also be in sufficient number and size to make boat handling enjoyable to all members of the crew or family. If the buyer hasn't enough experience to judge these features, he should secure the help of someone who is both honest and knowledgeable.

Ropes are a sailboat's very arteries. Their size, material, and condition are all-important. If the boat being considered for purchase is not well endowed in all rope departments, replacements will have to be purchased.

Sails are, naturally, the most important item in a sailboat's gear. They are its power plant. Their shape and condition are highly important to enjoyment of the boat. Always watch for worn places on edges, main expanse, or corners. Shape is very difficult to judge until the sails are seen on the boat with wind filling them out. Try to get an experienced sailor to guide you in judging sail shape.

These days, it would be difficult to buy any boat over twenty-five feet in length without an auxiliary engine. Most day-sailers and cruising boats under twenty-five feet are designed to accommodate an outboard engine. These engines are the modern adventurer's concession to the exigencies of calms and other threats to deadlines. The buyer who wants an engine should also inspect the mechanical contrivances serving as linkage: throttles, gear shifts, electrical circuitry, etc. Failure in any component means failure of the whole. Obviously, if a boat owner relies upon an engine that doesn't work, he is worse off than if he had none at all. Most people today know something about engines, but not enough to judge the quality and condition of marine engines and their accessories. Hence, prospective purchasers should seek the expert guidance of a marine mechanic. In addition to information on condition, get an expert's advice on the adequacy of the power for the job to be done—i.e., is the engine big enough to drive the boat in question?

Boat Size

It is not absolutely necessary for an adult to start in with a very small boat until he learns about sailing. The smaller the sailboat the quicker its responses, in general. In childhood years, quick boat responses usually make for quick skipper reactions. Kids learn more quickly and more thoroughly in boats that punish their mistakes by capsizing or otherwise embarrassing them. For the adult, such punishment may not fit the crime, but instead be drastic overkill.

With the passing of time, people seem to attain added capacity to correlate intellectual factors previously not experienced. However, in inverse proportion they have been losing the seat-of-the-pants, kinesthetic sensitivity characteristic of the young. Also, with the years they may have accumulated the fears and anxieties mentioned earlier. Consequently, adults are generally (rightly or wrongly) more interested in boats large enough to offer space, stability, and tame reaction times.

Boat Prices

Anyone who thinks in terms of bargains should look for old wooden boats and be prepared to spend a lot of time in maintenance. Some people enjoy working on boats, joiner work, painting, varnishing, caulking, and the like. In a boat of current design and assurable popularity, however, there is no such thing as a bargain—that is, one without a hidden flaw.

At the time this is written, good sailboats with all necessary gear start at around $550 new, and the really good ones depreciate very little and yield excellent values in the used boat market. In that price range are sailing dinghies and board boats. Prices go from there up to about $2500 for a 16-footer, and up to $20,000-plus for a 30-footer. There is no good rule of thumb on price per foot. In all but the most popular classes, used boat values are highly inconsistent.

Terms are available. However, as with houses, the best loan comes for the boat with the best resalability. Most prospective owners would do well to think as a bank does: even though I may like this boat now, could I sell it easily if I change my mind or circumstances change?

Perhaps the word "bargain" would take on a different aura if it were defined as "the most value for the dollar," instead of as "buying low." A bargain in boat buying means a boat which will yield the most enjoyment for the owner, cost only a reasonable amount to maintain over its life, and finally bring in the highest amount at resale. Such a boat is an investment.

Excellent publications listing all currently manufactured sailboats are available through *Sail* magazine, 38 Commercial Wharf, Boston, Massachusetts 02110 or *Yacht Racing,* 143 Rowayton Ave., Rowayton, Conn. 06853.

chapter 4

How to Board a Boat Safely

Boats may be berthed alongside a dock or in a slip, or they may be trailed, but a high percentage are kept at anchor or at a mooring, an arrangement requiring transportation across the intervening water, which may be a few feet or a few miles, but is mostly a few hundred yards. Affecting this fluid barrier are winds, waves, and tides. In and on it are boats, moving and stationary, and floats for mooring or anchor markers. As the demand for sailing and boats continues to grow, available water space in safe harbors may not allow for individual mooring or anchoring. This has already happened in a number of highly popular harbors, such as Wilmette, Illinois, where since the 1930s sailboats have been moored bow and stern or side by side and where pads must be hung out for protection against traffic. The space remaining barely allows the boats to sail out into the lake. However, as long as sailing is possible anywhere, sailors must know how to get their boats to water or to get across the water to their boats.

Trailing

Trailed boats eliminate the need for getting to the boat. One simply backs the trailer into the water, releases the boat, moves the car away, and goes for a sail. Of course, not all boats are trailable, but as the costs of dockage, moorings, and storage soar ever higher, more and more designs under thirty feet in length are capable of trailing.

There is no trick to trailing a boat. Just be sure to secure the boat carefully in the trailer and hitch the latter with care to the car. The hitching device itself must be well designed and well fastened to the car. Driving technique is no problem, as long as one drives forward; driving backward with a trailer is a skill all to itself. Note that most automobile insurance does not include trailing or objects being trailed without special riders.

At Dockside or in a Slip

A dock is a permanent structure available to boats on one, two, or three sides. A float is a dock which is fixed horizontally but free to rise and fall with the tide.

A slip is a small area reserved for a single boat (there can be many slips in a line abreast) and bounded by piles (poles driven into the harbor bottom). A boat is directed into this enclosed area and tied up to the piles and/or to the shore, adjoining the end of the slip. Typically, the piles alongside each side of the boat have walkways to get people and gear to shore. Other slips lack such walkways, and shore is attainable by jumping from the end of the boat facing the shore (usually the front end).

Clearly, slips and docks present no problem in getting to the boat. In this respect, they are ideal. Their problems arise when one must leave them under certain wind conditions, and this will be treated in Chapter 11.

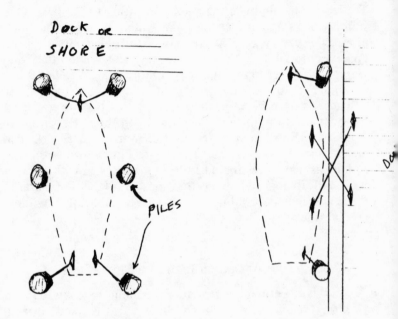

DOCK or SHORE

PILES

PILES

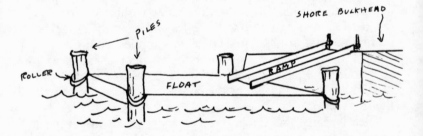

PILES

SHORE BULKHEAD

ROLLER

FLOAT

RAMP

Figure 4-1. *Top left:* Slip. *Top right:* Dock. *Bottom:* Float.

Rowing to a Mooring

The only remaining method of securing a boat is a mooring, which, in this chapter's connotation, is precisely the same as being at anchor. A mooring moves as the wind or tide moves the boat. A smaller boat—called a tender, skiff, row-boat, or dinghy—is usually employed for crossing the inter-vening water to the anchored or moored boat. Those owning outboard motors suited to dinghies (this name will be used henceforth) may wish to use them, particularly if the mooring is at some distance from the point of departure. However, skill in rowing will eliminate the need to rely on motors, which can be temperamental. The sailor of a moored boat should be able to row the dinghy to a reasonably far-out mooring in a strong cross wind and a tide-formed chop (a sloppy, short, steep wave form, difficult to row through and caused by tide running against waves). He should also be able to put the boat with its gear and passengers smoothly and safely alongside the sailboat for safe unloading.

Anyone who cannot row with skill enough to meet the qualifications noted above should take the time to learn that skill before trying to learn sailing. First things first.

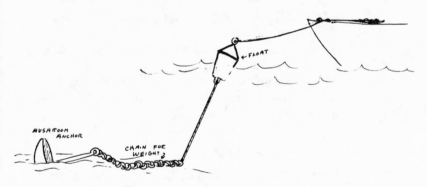

Figure 4-2. Mooring.

Of course, a rowboat needs a berth when not being used as a ferry. Yacht club members can usually rent float space quite reasonably. Others can find city-owned public rental floats or floats rented by marinas and boatyards. Car-top transportation from home, and garage or backyard storage while at home, constitute the least expensive dinghy handling ashore. When not in use, a dinghy should be turned bottom up to avoid the need for dumping out rain water. Owners who leave dinghies in public places should remove oars and rowlocks and lock them in the car trunk or other safe place.

En route from shore to sailboat, a sailor should keep his eyes well peeled for other boats, either moving or stationary. The boat density near docks, slips, and launching ramps can be formidable.

Nearing the sailboat, the oarsman must attempt to observe whether it is being wind-directed or tide-directed, because it is advisable to bring the dinghy alongside the larger boat so that the former faces the wind. This allows the wind to move the dinghy away from the larger boat and avoids chafing the latter's slick paint job. Even when the larger boat is tide-driven, the dinghy will go with the wind because it has a minuscule area available to the tide and a rather large area for the wind to grasp. Of course, if there is no wind the dinghy and the sailboat will yield to the tide alone. But with no wind there is no sailing anyway.

To facilitate unloading personnel and supplies, the dinghy may be tied temporarily alongside the sailboat. Thereafter, one can untie the tether and remove it to one end of the sailboat (usually the back), from which the dinghy will be blown to the end of its tether.

Boarding the Sailboat

A heavy keel boat will not react to the application of weight to one side as much as a light, centerboard boat will. The smaller and lighter the boat, the more care must be exercised in boarding her. This fact will have become evident during the trip in the dinghy to the sailboat. The oarsman will have noted that movement of weight from the center of the dinghy resulted in difficulty in rowing because of the tipping.

The closer to the sailboat's edge one initially steps, the more pronounced will be the tipping. Hence, people boarding small, light boats should step carefully as far toward the centerline as possible, whether embarking at dock, slip, or mooring. Also, in light sailboats one should be careful to get aboard at or near the widest part. Any attempt to board near the front end will very likely submerge that end. Also, the sailboat's lateral stability is lowest in front where the hull is narrowest.

Once one's weight is fully within the cockpit (sailing and handling area), that weight acts to stabilize the boat. However, any movement on deck for any purpose must be undertaken with a careful eye to weight distribution and its effects.

From studying a boat's reactions to weight changes while it is at dockside or on a mooring, one can learn much about how to move his weight when getting into it and rigging it as well as while sailing.

chapter 5

Putting Wind and Sails to Work

Of all the data comprising a weather report, to the sailor the most important are the direction and velocity of wind.

Wind is simply the mass motion of air, an invisible fluid which acts very much like other fluids, such as water. It flows from high places into low places. When warm, it rises; when cold, it sinks. It is deflected by obstructions, such as trees, houses, boats, and waves.

Without wind, a boat under sail alone cannot move (unless tide, another fluid force, is at work).

Wind, the Motive Power

Wind furnishes the motive power for sailing, but it complicates boat handling by causing wave motion, flying spray, tipping, and even capsizing (when a boat is ineptly handled or sailed in wind strengths unsuited to it). The skill, and most of the enjoyment, in sailing lies in acquiring the knack of maximizing the motive power while minimizing the hindrances.

The pressure of air moving against a sail varies as the square of the wind velocity. This means that doubling the wind velocity increases the wind force exerted on the sails, mast, and rig by a factor of four. Obviously, wind velocities are of great importance to the sailor.

Wind is inconstant. It is often contentious. However, it is the very essence of sailing, and the sailor must learn to tolerate it, even to like it. In fact, the wind's devilments help to satisfy man's atavistic need for elemental conquest.

Where to Get Weather Reports

There are two kinds of weather information helpful to sailors: (1) bulletins prepared for the general public, whose needs are simple and basic—whether to take a raincoat or not, what dress to wear, etc., and (2) marine bulletins analyzing current weather and adding forecasts for an area.

The bulletins in the first category are available via the nearest telephone; simply look up Weather Bureau under U.S. Government. Such forecasts are largely based on a computerized deduction statistically calculated from many past occasions featuring similar weather patterns. This deduction is often expressed as a percentage, e.g., "Today and tomorrow a 10 percent chance of precipitation," meaning that on the average, out of ten similar weather patterns, only one has yielded precipitation. If the computer proves to be wrong, it simply means that the high and low pressure areas, which dictate all weather, have moved faster or slower than they had in the patterns used to program the computer.

Where available, marine forecasts are the best source of information for sailors. They provide detailed information on wind direction, wind velocities, wave height and shape, and tidal movement, along with cloud cover and precipitation probabilities. These marine forecasts are available in areas where boating and/or fishing are popular sports, and they are broadcast over local radio stations periodically. It is important that all sailors learn the frequencies of such stations and the regularly scheduled times of the reports. Such information is available at boatyards, stores dealing in boat supplies, and the U.S. Coast Guard office.

Weather for Learning

Wind strength for inexperienced sailors should be ten miles per hour or lower. Such velocities propel a boat at a speed ample for rudder control and for enjoyment, but not great enough to cause serious damage in the event of mistakes. As the beginner acquires confidence—and most do after a very few hours of studious practice sessions—he can safely take on winds up to 16-18 miles per hour. However, the learner should remember that wind pressure at ten miles per hour is only one-fourth as strong as it is at twenty miles per hour.

In the initial hours of sailing, waves are almost as important as their parental winds, not only from a comfort standpoint but because of what they can do to steering and to the momentum of a boat while maneuvering. Even in light winds there may be waves left over from a recent storm, particularly if one is sailing at some distance from the windward shore. Wave height is predictable for a given wind force and water depth, but that predictable height is not realized until the wave has had a distance to build up, or fetch, as the nautical term has it.

Calm, which is the absence of wind velocity and pressure, leaves a sailboat a helpless, inanimate, drifting thing. If a becalmed sailboat is in a tidal current, it will drift until it breaks up in a collision or runs aground unless an anchor is thrown over to keep it put. An engine does not help one learn to sail, but it is a handy gadget in calm weather.

In any attempt to judge wind force, whether from smoke, flags, weather vanes, or waves, be very sure to watch something that is so located that the wind has an uninterrupted approach to it from a reasonably long distance. Also be sure that the air downwind from and at the altitude of the object observed has space to continue uninterrupted. Like water, air (wind) changes in both direction and velocity when obstructed in any way. Referring to the Beaufort Scale of Wind Force in this chapter will be helpful.

It pays to exercise caution in weather observation and selection. At the least, a sailor who goes out in his boat under unfavorable weather conditions may suffer personal embarrassment (the "rocking chair fleet" is inevitably present to witness any goofs); at the worst, he may incur damage to property and/or injury to self or others.

One of the best books written for sailors on meteorology in local areas is *Wind and Sailing Boats* by Alan Watts, Quadrangle Books, Chicago, 1967.

No-Man's-Land

The great majority of sailboats can sail only as close to the wind as approximately 45 degrees. This means that a segment of the horizon totaling 90 degrees (45 degrees on each side of wind source heading) is inaccessible to most sailboats at all times. This is a full 25 percent of the horizon. Hence, a full quarter of the sailing pie is "no-man's-land" to sailors. Yet today's sailors are fortunate, since not long ago square-riggers reckoned with a no-man's-land of 170 degrees, nearly half the pie. In modern contrast, the Twelve Meters, which compete for the America's Cup, can limit their verboten area to 60 degrees or less.

The Beaufort Scale of Wind Force*

Beaufort No.	General Description	Sea Criterion	Landsman's Criterion	Velocity In MPH
0	Calm	Sea like a mirror.	Smoke rises vertically	Less than 1
1	Light air	Ripples with the appearance of scales are formed, but without foam crests.	Direction of wind shown by smoke drift but not by wind vanes.	1 to 3
2	Light breeze	Small wavelets, still short but more pronounced. Crests have a glassy appearance and do not break.	Wind felt on face; leaves rustle; ordinary vane moved by wind.	4 to 7
3	Gentle breeze	Large wavelets. Crests begin to break. Foam of glassy appearance. Perhaps scattered white horses.	Leaves and small twigs in constant motion. Wind extends light flags.	8 to 12
4	Moderate breeze	Small waves becoming longer; fairly frequent white horses.	Wind raises dust and loose paper; small branches are moved.	13 to 18
5	Fresh breeze	Moderate waves, taking a more pronounced long form; many white horses are formed. Chance of some spray.	Small trees in leaf begin to sway. Crested wavelets form on inland waters.	19 to 24
6	Strong breeze	Large waves begin to form; the white foam crests are more extensive everywhere. Probably some spray.	Large branches in motion; whistling heard in telegraph wires, umbrellas used with difficulty.	25 to 31

7	Near gale	Whole trees in motion; inconvenience felt when walking against wind.	Sea heaps up and white foam from breaking waves begins to be blown in streaks along the direction of the wind.	32 to 38
8	Gale	Wind breaks twigs off trees; generally impedes progress.	Moderately high waves of greater length; edges of crests begin to break into spindrift. The foam is blown in well-marked streaks along the direction of the wind.	39 to 46
9	Strong gale	Slight structural damage occurs (chimney pots and shingles removed).	High waves. Dense streaks of foam along the direction of the wind. Crests of waves begin to topple, tumble and roll over. Spray may affect visibility.	47 to 54
10	Storm	Seldom experienced inland; trees uprooted; considerable structural damage occurs.	Very high waves with long overhanging crests. The resulting foam in great patches is blown in dense white streaks along the direction of the wind. On the whole, the surface takes on a white appearance. The tumbling of the sea becomes heavy and shocklike. Visibility affected.	55 to 63

* Wind strength has always been very difficult to assess at sea, where waves and boat heeling make velocities seem greater than they really are. In 1806 Admiral Beaufort designed a scale for judging wind strength at sea. His criteria were intended for use by the captains of naval ships of the era and hence are not applicable today as originally written. The above sea criteria have been agreed upon by international meteorological organizations since 1939 and amended in the light of expert experience. The landsman's criteria are much older, having been devised in 1906 and having stood the test of time to date. In many versions of the Scale two additional categories appear, up to Hurricane, above 72 mph. However, for the purposes of this book, ten would seem sufficient.

The Importance of Wind Direction

In the art of sailing, the single most important factor to be reckoned with is wind direction. The sailor must have a continuing awareness of where the wind is coming from.

Sailors' language describing wind direction uses three-dimensional words in a two-dimensional way. Thus, "upwind," "above," "high," and "over" all mean toward the wind; while "downwind," "below," "low," and "under" mean away from the wind. Because a boat's front end is normally pointed toward the wind, "over the bow" means ahead of the boat, while "under the stern" means behind the boat.

Wind direction is the controlling factor in determining the courses in which a boat may sail, and in the adjustment of its sails to make those courses good. Only the sure knowledge of wind direction can enable a sailor to handle his boat so as to pacify the forces the wind can exert and to turn them in his favor.

Wind described as a compass direction (ESE or 260 degrees, etc.) is not nearly so important in sailing as wind direction described in terms which relate to the angles of the boat and the sail to that wind. This alignment is the basis for both driving and stopping a sailboat.

When Sails Are "in Neutral"

When the front edge of a sail faces the wind, that sail is "in neutral" because the wind can slip past both surfaces of the sail with equal pressure and therefore cannot push it into a driving shape in either direction. The leading edge of a sail is fastened to a vertical member of the boat, mast, or mast stay (wire holding the mast rigid). Hence, even with sails raised, the boat itself is also "in neutral" as long as the back edge of the sail is unfettered and free to go where the wind directs. A boat can remain "in neutral" with the sails angled as much from the centerline as 80 degrees or more. Obviously, knowing when a boat is in neutral (lacking forward motion exerted by the sails) is a prime requisite to knowing how to stop the boat safely. Sailboats have no brakes or reverse gears.

Since a boat cannot utilize wind power when the sail faces the wind, such power can be employed only by angling the sail from the wind. Any combination of angles—sail to boat and sail to wind—which enables the sail to fill with wind from one side only will set the boat in motion.

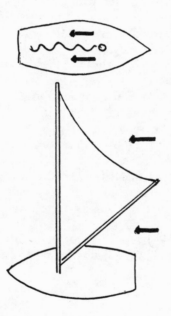

Figure 5-1. *Top:* Wind striking both sides of sail, generating no power. *Bottom:* Wind striking one side of sail only, generating power.

How to Locate Wind Direction

To help tell where the wind is coming from (wind direction), there are many aids—flags, smoke, boats at anchor or at moorings, waves, weather vanes on shore or on boats, ribbons or pieces of yarn on one's own boat or neighboring craft, etc. However, the very best technique—best because it is always available—is to develop a consciousness of the sensitivity of one's skin in any area exposed to the wind, mostly in the face, neck, and head. A normal person's skin is sufficiently sensitive to feel the slightest breeze. The idea is to concentrate on the definite cooling effect noted on the skin surface directed toward the wind. However, the too-often used technique of pointing a wet finger is misleading, since the entire finger is wet and evaporation causes coolness *away* from the wind as well as toward it.

The most effective techniques are these:

1) Turn your nose toward the wind in general. Move your head from side to side until the coolness is felt equally on both sides of your nose and until the sound of the wind is heard equally in both ears. At this point, your nose is accurately facing the wind.

2) Use a good masthead fly (weather vane on top of the mast). It is an invaluable tool for experts as well as beginners.

In time you will learn to read wind direction from the water's motion, but this can be confusing at the outset.

The Apparent Wind

From any stationary location wind direction is easy to define. However, on a moving platform another factor enters the equation, namely, the wind caused by the movement of that platform.

Wind is air in motion. Moving a platform through motionless air sets the air in motion, and hence causes wind. Everyone has watched the flags on a vessel moving in calm air; they stream back, in opposite direction to that of the vessel's heading. When the true (ambient) wind and the motion-caused wind are present at the same time, they produce a wind force and wind direction, the "apparent wind." Obviously, there cannot be two separate winds on board a sailboat; so the sailor will see and feel only the apparent wind in every condition other than a flat calm. The boat, sails, vanes, and telltales will also react only to the apparent wind.

The apparent wind constantly varies with the speed of the boat and the shifts and changing velocities of the true wind. Fortunately, the sailor does not often have to analyze these factors; he must deal only with their result, the apparent wind.

When the boat is sailing close to the wind, at an angle of forty-five degrees, the apparent wind's velocity will be the *sum* of much of the true wind and *all* of the motion wind— yielding a very marked increase in fresh breezes, when *both* wind velocity and boat velocity are increased. Conversely, when the boat sails with a following wind, the velocity of the apparent wind is the *difference* between the velocities of the true and the motion wind. Since the boat, in effect, is trying to run away from the wind, the resultant impression is one of relative calm; the wind powering the sail is of far lower velocity than it is when the boat sails close to the wind. For this reason, spinnakers, those beautiful and very large sails, were developed. When the boat is sailing at an angle to the wind between forty-five degrees and a downwind course, the apparent wind velocity will decrease as the angle of the boat to the wind increases.

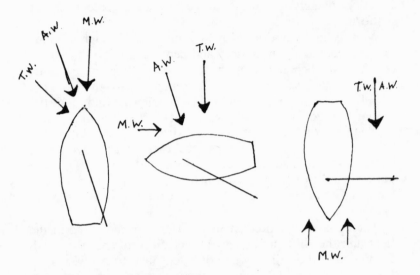

Figure 5-2. The apparent wind.
In the diagram, T.W. stands for the true wind, A.W. for the apparent wind, and
M.W. for the motion wind. From left to right, the drawings show the relationship
of the apparent wind to the true and motion winds in beating, reaching, and running, respectively.

Wind shifts occur with far greater frequency than do
changes in boat speed, but boat speed does change apparent
wind direction. In non-technical terms, the harder the wind
blows, the nearer to the direction of the true wind is the apparent wind. Conversely, the faster the boat sails, the closer
to the boat's heading the apparent wind moves. Thus, when
there is a temporary lull in the wind, the boat may still be
driving fast as a result of the last gust, and the apparent wind
will move toward the bow. When the next gust arrives, it will
force the apparent wind back from the bow and toward the
direction of the true wind. These facts are most important
when sailing close to the wind, because in the effort to get as

close as possible to the wind, the observant sailor will steer a bit closer to the destination on every gust but must steer slightly away from that destination on the lulls.

Sail Shape and Design

Modern sails are universally triangular. Since the 1920s it has been known that the forward third of a sail generates a disproportionately high percentage of the total driving power of that sail. Hence, masts became taller in order to get a longer forward third.

Sailors learned in the 1920s that sails angled toward or across the wind derive 60-75 percent of their power from the surface away from the wind, in the form of "low pressure" or suction. In fact, a sail is an airfoil, just as is an airplane wing, which lifts the plane by lower pressure on the upper surface. As in all airfoils, this lower pressure is a function of the curve designed into the surface away from the wind in a sailboat, on top in a plane. Neither a sail nor wing could derive much pressure differential if its surface were flat. It is the location and depth of this curve which controls the efficiency of a sail.

A given hull is designed to be driven by sails with rather carefully calculated areas, most being shaped with one very long side and a relatively short base, or with a shorter height which for a given area requires a longer base. The designer selects sail dimensions to satisfy requirements for stability and/or speed for the hull it will drive.

A boat will sail with poor sails, but it will not sail efficiently, and it will be more difficult to handle.

There are many sailboat rigs—yawls, schooners, cutters, sloops, and catboats, to name the most popular. The smallest boats available, those in the 7-12 foot category, are catboats. (Catboats have never been large, topping out in their heyday at around 40 feet.) However, above 12-14 feet, most boats under 40 feet are sloops. Only occasionally does one find a yawl, ketch, or schooner under 40 feet. For people starting to sail, catboats and sloops are at once the easiest to buy, sell, and sail. A normally designed sloop can be sailed without the small sail, "cat-rigged" as the saying goes, thereby making it almost as easy to handle as a catboat.

Sail Adjustment*

With the sail on one side, a boat may be pointed throughout an arc from a 45-degree angle, the closest possible to the wind, to 180 degrees, pointing directly away from the wind. Since the sail can obviously be located on either side, the same arc is available with the wind coming from either side of the boat. Simply changing the heading of a boat within the prescribed arcs, however, will not alone cause that boat to move off in the desired direction. The sail must assert its power, and it can do so only when it is properly angled to the wind. For instance, to sail as close as possible to the wind, locate the sail as close as efficiently possible to the boat's centerline. When steering directly downwind, move the sail out away from the centerline as far as efficiently possible, between 80 and 90 degrees. For every course between the two mentioned there is a fitting sail location, and you must adjust the position of the sail to the course so that the boat can develop its optimum drive. For each course farther from the wind, release the sail farther from the centerline. For each course closer to the wind, pull the sail closer to the centerline. There are rules of thumb for effecting these adjustments efficiently, and these rules will be noted in Chapter 8.

---

*Use of the learning aids illustrated in Figure 8-8 will assist the reader in understanding this section.

chapter 6

Understanding Rigging and Hardware

Compared to the complexities of the old square-riggers, even the most sophisticated racing craft in modern sailing is a model of simplicity. However, to the uninitiated the simplest sailboat might at first appear complex.

The larger the boat the stronger and more extensive the whole rig must be; obviously, there are more individual items in boats with several sails as compared to a catboat. However, basic components found in the smallest, simplest boat will also be found in the most complicated boat, because, no matter what the size of the vessel, it must have a hull, one or more sails, one or more rigid (or semirigid) poles to spread the sail cloth, ropes to pull the sails up and to adjust their angle, and hardware for guiding and fastening those ropes.

There are two kinds of rigging: standing and running. There are two kinds of rope: wire and fiber. There are basically three categories of hardware: leading or guiding devices, devices to fasten ropes or other hardware to, and sliding devices for the controlled movement of ropes and/or sails.

Standing Rigging

This category covers the wires and pertinent fittings for holding the mast upright in the boat. The mast is supported by wires called "stays," just as the poles or high-wire apparatus inside a circus tent are supported by guy wires. In very small boats, whose mast size is sufficient by itself to maintain its strength, no standing rigging is necessary. Catboats in all sizes of the old quadrilateral sail type use little, if any, standing rigging. Sloops and other rigs from about fourteen feet up use the following:

1) One stay leading from top of mast, or near the top, to the boat's front end.

2) One or more wires, called "shrouds" or "side stays," leading on each side from the mast to the sides of the boat. If there is more than one shroud, one or more will lead from a point lower on the mast than its top.

3) One stay from the top of the mast to the boat's back end, or one backstay on each side from well up on the mast to a point on the deck well back on the boat.

With the exception of the backstay, the last item mentioned, which is adjustable while sailing, standing rigging is so named because it is seldom adjusted after the boat is "tuned" for sailing efficiency at the beginning of the season.

The shrouds are led over the ends of rigid, strutlike "spreaders" made of wood or aluminum, which strengthen the support for the mast by increasing the angle between the mast and the upper part of each shroud (see Fig. 6-1).

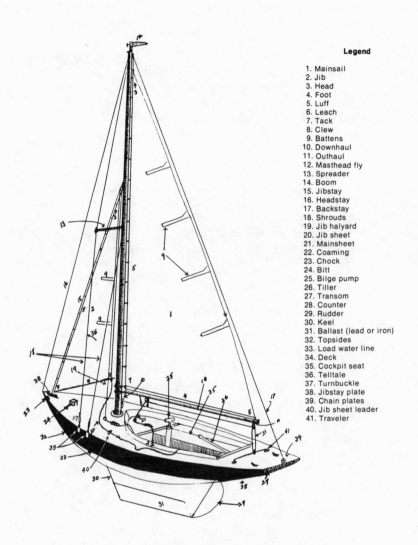

Figure 6-1. Sail plan and deck layout of typical keel knockabout.

The lower ends of all permanent stays are fitted with turn-buckles which allow for a few inches adjustment of stay length.

Figure 6-1 shows the standing and running rigging and the deck layout of a typical keel knockabout. The deck layout of a centerboard boat of similar size would be the same except that in the center of the cockpit would be a "box" in which the board is housed when pulled up.

Running Rigging

In this category are all the ropes used to raise and lower sails, to adjust the angle of the sails to the boat, and to adjust sail shape. As contrasted with the standing rigging which is susceptible to only minor adjustment, running rigging is highly adjustable and is being "run" in and out much of the time.

Running rigging is made of wire or fiber. In boats over fourteen feet ropes used to raise sails are usually made of wire to which rope is spliced. This is to make it easy on the sailor's hands when he is pulling on it.

Materials Used in Rigging

Wire rope for yachts is almost universally stainless steel, for both strength and long life. For standing rigging this wire consists of a single strand of nineteen smaller wires twisted together. Such wire is rather stiff and inflexible.

Wire used in running rigging is also made of stainless steel, but it consists of three or more strands, each made of a number of smaller wires, twisted together. This type is flexible, as is necessary for any material to be run around blocks or through leads.

Fiber rope is available in sisal, manila (hemp), linen, dacron, nylon, and polypropylene. Of these, the least expensive is sisal, the most expensive dacron. However, for freedom from problems such as mildew, ease on the sailor's hands, and longest life, dacron is the best value. (Nylon has an advantage as anchor rope because of its high stretchability.) Dacron may be bought in three- or four-ply lays, or as braid. The latter is easiest on the hands for ropes used often, such as those for adjusting sail angle.

Hardware is available in galvanized steel, stainless steel, or bronze. High strength to weight is important. Of the three materials mentioned, galvanized steel is the lowest in both price and strength to weight ratio, while stainless steel is the highest in both categories. Unless one enjoys polishing bronze, which is a good material for most hardware, stainless steel is often the best value. It needs little attention and has strength enough to make small-sized, low weight hardware possible. Bronze is often chrome-plated, but the plating has a limited life around salt water, particularly where its surface is used for any abrasive purpose. such as leading or tying rope. Synthetic materials have lately begun to widen the selection potential. These new, tough plastics are used to replace the more familiar wood and metal in pulleys, cleats, and winches. More and more, through the discoveries made in racing competition, sophisticated plastics and metals are appearing in the supply stores at reasonable prices for the weekend sailor.

Blocks and Winches

Leading or guiding devices lead rope or change its direction from one place to another via a route handiest for the sailor and can also increase the sailor's pulling power. They are found in two forms: simple shapes used for leading or guiding only, or pulleys with one or more wheels for both leading and increasing pulling power. Pulleys known as "blocks" have a variety of shapes and functions: "cheek blocks" which mount permanently and flat on a deck or a spar; blocks with "beckets," which are devices on one end of the block to which a thimble or shackle may be fastened; "snatch blocks," which include a snap hook for quick fastening to a pad or thimble, etc.

Winches are fittings which increase pulling power. Wrapping a rope several times around a drum, using a long handle for leverage in turning that drum, makes a large amount of "purchase" available. Winch drums are fitted with pawls which allow their turning only in a clockwise direction, so that when winding the drum one doesn't lose what he has pulled because of back-turning. The more turns of rope on the drum, the more friction and hence holding power the sailor will acquire.

Fastening Devices

Devices for fastening ropes are hooks, shackles, and cleats.

Hooks are almost all closable by means of a spring-loaded snap or a hinged crook with a spring-loaded pin which fits into a hole in the main part to close. Such hooks are termed "snap hooks."

Shackles are all approximately U-shaped and all have pins of one design or another across the legs of the U for secure closing. Some are "snap shackles" which feature a quick opening and closing design very similar to that of the snap hook. Others have simple threaded pins which are screwed in for closure. Still others have key-shaped pins which fit precisely through a matching aperture and are turned for closure.

Devices to which ropes are fastened are called "cleats" and "bitts." Cleats are of three main types, the standard, the cam and clam cleat, the last without spring-loaded jaws.

Standard cleats are shaped something like a short T with a very long crossbar. A rope is led under one arm of the T, crossed back over the arm, and led under the other arm. This procedure is repeated several times for needed friction. Thus a figure-eight pattern is developed.

Cam cleats are used where a rope is likely to be adjusted quite often. The rope leads between two serrated jaws which are spring-loaded to close on it. As the rope moves through, the jaws open, but are forced by their springs onto the rope, which is then held in place by the serrations. To loose the rope requires only lifting it out of the jaws. Such cleats are quick and yet sure.

Bitts are posts with a pin through them to which rope is fastened.

Devices to fasten other hardware to are thimbles and pads, such as deck plates with eyes in them to receive thimbles or shackles. A thimble is a pear-shaped or round fitting used for providing eye splices (spliced loops) in rope with the hardness to protect them from chafe in use. Pads are mounted on deck or on masts or other spars. Other rather specialized fittings in this category are the gooseneck and chain plates. A gooseneck is the universal joint which fastens the pole (spar) at the bottom of the mainsail to the mast. (From now on this bottom pole will be referred to by its correct name, "boom.") Chain plates are metal plates bolted to the side of sailboats for fastening the stays that support the mast.

Sliding Devices

Sliding devices permit a fitting, such as a block, pad, or stay, to be moved from one location to another where the distance for such movement is short and where the primary need is to keep the adjustment along a single plane. Such a device would be the track on which movable backstay slides move, or the track to which is led the rope for controlling the jib or front sail. Lighter weight track is used on many masts to carry sail slides which in turn are attached to the long front edge of the mainsail. The slide-and-track arrangement is one which permits raising the sail and holding its edge close to the mast when raised. Such devices take the place of hoops that were used in former times.

A Sailboat's Layout

There is an infinite variety in the location of rigging and hardware components, but differences in the components themselves are small. Once a sailor understands the functions of the fixtures in one boat, he will know what to look for in any sailboat of any size. Reference to Figure 6-1, showing a typical layout of a keel knockabout in the 14-40 foot range, will help the reader understand the following discussion of boat layout.

Starting at the front end (bow, pronounced "bough"), one first finds the headstay (foremost stay), then the jibstay fastened to the jibstay plate.

On either side of the bow is a leading device with two prongs, often overlapping. This is called a "chock" and is for guiding towlines and anchor lines.

One corner of the small sail used ahead of the mast is fastened to the jibstay plate fitting.

Still on the centerline but behind this fitting is a cleat or bitt for securing the anchor or towline.

Behind this cleat or bitt is the mast itself.

Laterally opposite the mast are the shroud (side stay) chain plates, one or more of them somewhat back of the mast, although at the edge of the hull.

On the mast of some boats are cleats, blocks, leaders, and/or winches for handling lines which adjust mainsail shape and raise the sails. Each such line requires a cleat, and if not on the mast, these are back of the mast and handy to working from the cockpit. The small boat in the illustration needs no winches, and the cleats and leaders are on deck.

Also near the mast are blocks or leaders for the rope which adjusts the angle of the front sail.

Sometimes winches are found on deck, back of the mast and handy to the cockpit. These might be for raising sail or for adjusting sail angles.

If the boat has a centerboard, it is immediately obvious. Centerboards are housed in "boxes" on the boat's centerline, usually just behind the front edge of the cockpit. The box is quite long, of a height nearly that of the deck, and quite thin. The board is hinged at the lower front corner and on small boats is adjusted in depth by a handle; on larger boats a rope-and-block arrangement furnishes the needed increment in pulling power. In small boats with dagger boards the box is open at the top and the board is lowered vertically into the box, much as a dagger fits into its sheath.

When used, adjustable backstays terminate alongside the cockpit on each side of the deck, using a bar track and a sliding device which holds the stay (none is shown in the illustration). A permanent backstay terminates at a chain plate at the very back end of the boat.

Near the back end of the cockpit, or behind it, is a transverse arrangement called a traveler, on which the mainsail's adjusting line is allowed to slide from side to side. This arrangement may be a wire or a bar track. In either case the line is hooked to it via a block which does the sliding.

On both sides of the cockpit may be winches for handling the adjusting lines for large front sails.

Toward the back of the cockpit, or sometimes at the very back end of the boat, is the rudder post to which the tiller is fastened. The tiller is a lever usually made of wood and used for steering. It is mounted to the post on a hinged fitting which enables the helmsman to raise the tiller if desired when he changes position in the cockpit.

Boats with steering wheels usually have these sufficiently far ahead of the back edge of the cockpit to enable the helmsman to stand behind them. Out of sight every wheel operates a small tiller (helm) just as does the helmsman (gearing increases power to allow the use of such short tillers for wheel actuation).

Fastening devices for the line which adjusts the mainsail angle may be found in a variety of locations—ahead of the cockpit, behind it, in it, etc. However, this line is easy to spot since it must lead up to the boom.

On the boom itself are blocks, leaders, and cleats for handling lines to adjust sail shape.

Knots and Ties

Each among the thousands of knots included in any good book on the subject is a unique device for securing a piece of rope to another object. Many are specific and limited in utility, others are decorative and not utilitarian, and still others are of general usefulness. The work of all nondecorative knots is done by friction alone.

The five knots discussed below have general utility. Further, they are all very easy to untie under all conditions, a great asset when time is of the essence, as it often is. Figure 6-2 includes one drawing for each of the five knots, plus the lark's head and granny, which are the wrong ways of tying the clove hitch and reef knot, respectively.

Bowline (pronounced "bō′lǐn"). To form a secure loop in the end of a piece of line. Can also be used when fastening the ends of two pieces of line together; simply use a bowline in each end.

Two Half Hitches. One of the simplest. Used to fasten the end of one piece of line to itself after forming a loop around a post, another piece of line, etc.

Clove Hitch. Similar to two half hitches but used in the middle of a piece of line to secure it to a post or other line.

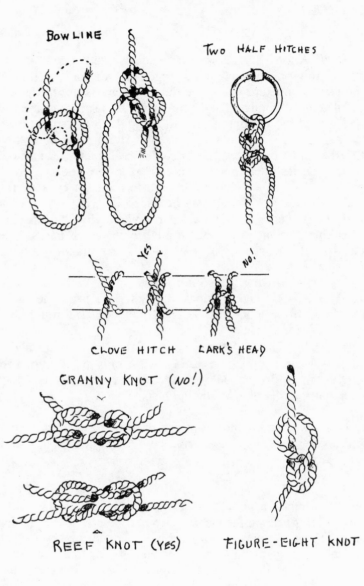

Figure 6-2. Useful knots.

Reef Knot. Sometimes erroneously called a "square knot," this one is used to tie together two ends of line of the same diameter. The name derives from its use to tie reef points (short lengths of light line sewn into sails and used to furl part of the bottom of the sail along the boom to diminish the sail area). To maintain its strength, both ropes being tied together must be under pressure. The reef knot will not hold its friction if either rope end is moved toward the knot after tying; in fact, this technique is used to untie, or capsize, the knot. Additional security may be added by tying a half hitch with the free ends on the main part. When tying, be sure that ends emerge from the knot parallel to the main part of the line (part bearing the load). The other way makes a granny knot, of no value at all.

Figure-eight Knot. This knot is used at the end of any line which is led through a block or leader, to keep the line's bitter end from being inadvertently pulled back through that block or leader.

Naturally, knowledge of many knots is both useful and a source of pleasure. However, knowing only the five named above will equip the sailor to secure himself and his vessel from harm under almost all circumstances.

Ties are used for the following purposes: (1) to tie a line onto a cleat or bitt, (2) to form a coil, (3) to hang a coil, and (4) to stow a line.

To Tie a Line onto a Cleat or Bitt. Leaving enough line length to make a number of turns around the cleat or bitt, bring the line along the cleat or around the bitt, turn it under and then back across, thus starting what will be a series of figure-eights over and around. When three or four such frictions have been developed, force the end of the line under the other turns, if that line may need to be freed quickly; or, make one half hitch around one end of the cleat or one end of

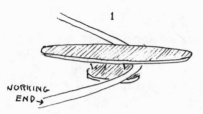

1

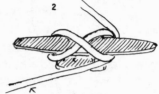

2

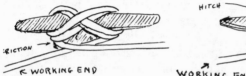

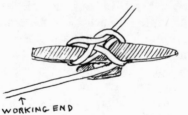

Figure 6-3. Tying a line onto a cleat.
Top: How to start a line onto a cleat. *Left center:* For quick release the line is "frictioned" between the figure-eight turns on the cleat and the "working part"
which has the tension (left side). *Right center:* For maximum friction turn the line
over in a hitch to finish the tie. Note that the hitch must finish with the loose end
(right side) lying parallel to the figure-eight turn. *Bottom:* If the hitch is made backward, not parallel, its holding power is almost nil.

a bitt crossbar, if the line is to be left for a time and will not need fast untying. To hold, the hitch must end up so that the rope end lies parallel to, not across, the turn on the cleat under it.

To Form a Coil. On a sailboat the entire unused length of any line should at all times be formed into a coil and so located that the line can be ready for immediate use. There is a correct way to form a coil and to keep it ready.

If you are righthanded, hold the line in the left hand a short distance from its fastening point, if only part of it is being used (such as a halyard or sheet), or at one end if entirely free (such as a jib sheet to be coiled for stowing). Assuming that the line is around ½-¾ inch in diameter, slide the right hand along the line until that hand is 2-4 feet from the left hand (coil diameters vary with line diameter). With the right hand bring that 2-4 feet of line back to the left hand, thus forming a loop; then transfer the loop to the left hand. Repeat this series of actions until the entire line is in a series of loops held in the left hand. The distance traveled along the line by the right hand controls the coil diameter; and if that distance is the same for each loop, the entire coil will be uniform in diameter. The loops are made clockwise. Dacron tends to form figure-eights instead of round loops. There is no harm in coiling with figure-eights, but if the sailor prefers a round coil, he can form one by allowing the fingers of the right hand to twist the line about a quarter-turn clockwise as each loop is formed; this will remove the figure-eight.

Whenever a coil is laid down in readiness for use, it must be placed so that the end to be pulled is on top.

To Hang a Coil. This tie applies only to lines in use—halyards, sheets, etc. Leaving about 2-3 feet of the line free at the cleat end, form the coil; then make a loop of the free segment and pull that loop through the coil. Then through that loop pull a second loop made from the remainder of the free segment, and hang this final loop over the cleat. When you

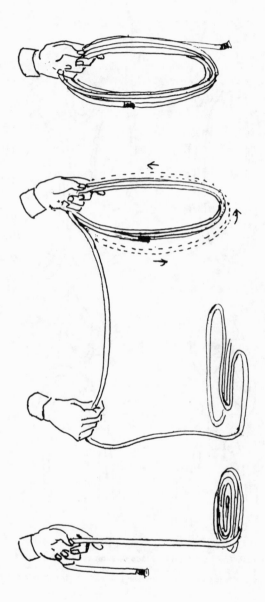

Figure 6-4. Forming a coil.

Left: If you are righthanded, start with your left hand at one end of an idle coil, or at the working end of a line in use. *Center:* Slide right hand along line to a point that allows line enough for a coil turn. Return that point to left hand. *Right:* Repeat this operation until entire line is in left hand.

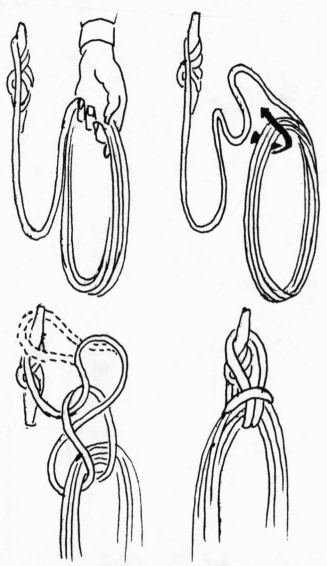

Figure 6-5. Hanging a coil.
Top left: Form the coil. *Top right:* Pull one loop through coil. *Bottom left:* Pull second loop through first loop. *Bottom right:* Hang coil on cleat by this second loop. (Note that both loops are taken from line between coil and cleat, *not* from the loose end.)

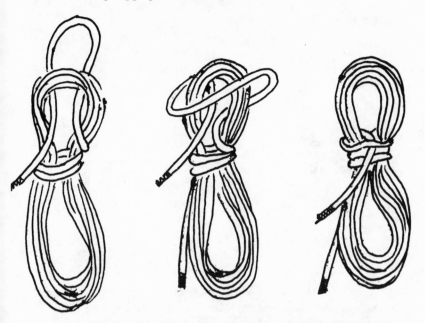

Figure 6-6. Stowing a line.
To stow a coil so that it is compact and also can be loosed quickly for use, follow the steps shown above in order from left to right. *Left:* Wrap 2-3 turns around finished coil; then pull loop through coil. *Center:* Slip loop down over top of coil. *Right:* Pull the end tight. (Note that some line must be held back from the coil for the loop.)

wish to use the halyard again, you can free the entire coil by lifting it from the cleat and pulling straight back.

To Stow a Line. When leaving the boat to go ashore, there may be several lines to stow—dock lines, jib sheets, etc. Starting with an end, proceed to coil as described above until only about 2-3 feet remain at the other end. Make 2-3 turns around the squeezed-together coil; then pull a loop through the coil and thence over an end of the coil. Tighten down on the loop by pulling the short end, and the coil will be neat and secure, yet easy to undo quickly.

chapter 7

Steering a Course

As compared with steering a car, steering vehicles in a fluid has similarities (often indiscernible) and dissimilarities (quite discernible when one looks for them).

Understanding both similarities and dissimilarities is a prerequisite to boating, since steering is clearly a most important function of control. At the very least, faulty steering will slow the boat down; at most, it will damage people and property.

How a Rudder Works

Every boat has a rudder. A rudder is the submerged device almost always located near the back end of the boat and designed to deflect the flow of water so as to turn the boat. Sailboats can be steered by the skillful adjustment of sails alone. However, this is doing it the hard way; and if one has the skill to do that, he has long since relegated rudder knowledge to his subconscious.

A boat's rudder action is quite different from that of a car's front wheels, though both may be directed by a turn of a steering wheel. In a car, when the driver desires to turn right, he turns the steering wheel clockwise, thus causing the front wheels to turn clockwise, or to the right. The car itself follows the wheels in the clockwise direction even though momentum tends to maintain prior direction and is cancelled only by the friction of tires on road surface. However, in a boat, when the skipper desires to turn right, he must rotate the rudder to the right side of the centerline. This action deflects the flow of water caused by the boat's forward motion. It interrupts the water flow and directs it toward the hull, thereby pushing the boat's back end to the left. Since there is no friction, such as between vehicle and road, when the back end skids to the left the front end goes right, and the turn is accomplished. As in a car, hard, quick turns increase the skid and diminish speed. The best turns are made with an easy but definite motion.

In a fluid a vehicle tends to turn on an axis near its center of gravity, which, in a boat, is close to its middle. Thus, the back end swings as much as the front end, contrasting with a friction-bound car, which "tracks" in pursuit of its front wheels. This movement from a given course must be taken into consideration when in a normal turn the back end of a boat may move toward a hazardous object on a collision course (see Fig. 7-1). This means that when the skipper turns his boat *away from* an object, the boat's back end will actually turn *toward* that object.

If a rudder works by deflecting the flow of water caused by the vessel's forward motion, it follows that with no forward motion there can be no steering. Similarly, the rudder works more efficiently when the speed of the boat is high than it does when that speed is slow. At top speed, rudder action is fast and positive. At slow speed, it is sluggish. This fact dictates a varying technique in rudder control. When the boat is

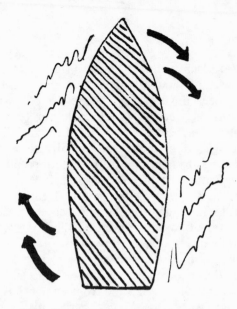

Figure 7-1. How a boat swivels during a turn.
A boat swivels around its center of gravity during a turn. The back end swings one way, the front end the other way.

moving at top speed, only a slight movement of the rudder is needed to effect a normally fast turn of the boat. At slow speed the rudder must be pushed much farther across the boat to get the same result in turning. In the exercises outlined in Chapter 9, you can very quickly learn the steering "personality" of your own boat in different wind velocities and at different points of sailing.

The Steering Wheel

Some sailors prefer the wheel over the tiller, because although a wheel does not transmit the "feel" of the boat as a tiller does, it stays put better when one wishes relief from a steering stint. In a boat a steering wheel works with precisely the same turning effect as it does in a car, except for the swiveling of the boat's back end, which is the same no matter what sort of device works the rudder.

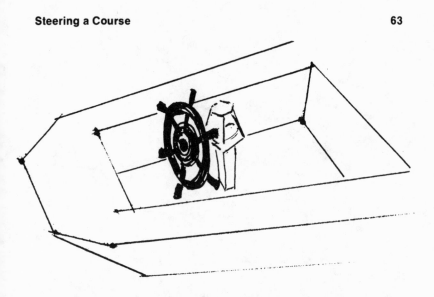

Figure 7-2. Steering wheel.

Wheels are found in very few boats of overall lengths less than thirty feet. They are used mainly in the larger boats because as size increases so does loading on the rudder, which transmits this loading directly to the sailor via a tiller, whereas the linkages between wheel and rudder absorb it.

The Tiller

One new discipline required of all newcomers to small sailboats is that of steering by tiller. A tiller is a leverlike stick fastened at one end to the rudder post (see Fig. 7-3). When one wishes to turn the rudder to the right, the tiller must be turned left. At the outset it is necessary to go through the intellectual nuisance of saying to one's self: "Tiller left, boat turns right. Tiller right, boat turns left." Fortunately, it does not take long to turn this bugaboo into reflex action.

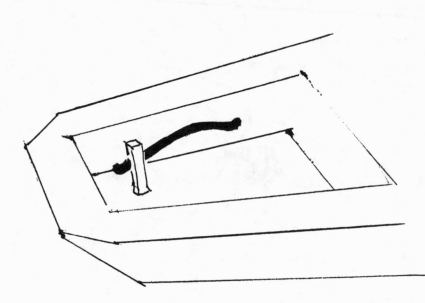

Figure 7-3. Tiller.

Often beginners have a tendency to pull the tiller inadvertently when they move their head or body away from normal steering position, and to push it when they move toward that position and beyond. This is similar to the phenomenon some of us can remember when learning to drive: when we turned our heads to the left, we would turn the wheel to the left. The sailor must learn to keep his tiller hand in neutral even when his body or head is moving.

Another common failing of novices is that they often sit much too far back in the boat and with the tiller rigidly clamped under the armpit. This tendency must be squelched before it becomes a bad habit that the sailor will have to unlearn. The helmsman should sit comfortably erect forward of the arc described by the end of the tiller.

A beginner often grasps the tiller with a five-finger, white-knuckled clutch. Such a grip needlessly wastes energy. It is far more efficient to use the ends of two or three fingers and guide the tiller with easy motions.

Parallax

Defined as "the apparent change in the position of an object resulting from the change in the direction or position from which it is viewed," parallax becomes a factor in sailing only because the normal position of the steersman using a tiller is away from the centerline of the boat—on deck or at closest on a seat. (Using a wheel allows steering on the centerline.) It seems to be a fairly general tendency to aim at a destination object by lining that object up with the headstay or other fitting at the bow. If no compensation is made for the aimer's location off the centerline, the boat's course will deviate several degrees from the intended route. The solution is a mental effort to aim with a part of the boat approximately as far off center as is the aimer. In a few trips this compensation becomes quite unconscious.

Tides and Currents

Since tidal current often influences steering, it is treated in this chapter.

Anyone planning to sail in lakes will not experience the rise and fall of tides. However, in waters open to the sea, the gravitational pull of sun and moon causes these waters to move. The result is lower water levels where the pull is from, and higher levels where the pull is to. Coupled with changes in level are the currents which mark the movement of the water bodies.

Tidal rise and fall is predictable in time and extent, except when unusually high winds augment or subtract from nature's rhythms. The sailor can buy charts for currents and will find tidal rise and fall data in any waterfront newspaper.

Current is important to the navigator, since it can increase or diminish speed "made good," and when flowing across one's course will require direction changes to counteract deviation from the desired track.

Throughout the world tidal rise and fall vary from zero to over fifty feet. However, most harbors you are likely to visit will have a range of two to ten feet.

In most locations, the tide takes just over six hours to come in, another six to go out, and so on, thus making two complete cycles each day.

In a tidal situation where the rise and fall is three feet in its allotted six hours, an observer would need to watch for most of an hour to note changes in level. It would take this much time for the ramp angle to change, for the rocks on shore to be covered or uncovered, or for shoal spots to appear or disappear. However, in a long afternoon sail the changes can be dramatic and must be watched for.

On a chart the depths shown are in "mean low water," meaning the mean figure computed from low water figures over an extended period of time. Tidal lows and highs are by no means the same each day. Twice each month, for instance, there are days when rise and fall are markedly greater than the mean (spring tides). At other periods each month the highs and lows are much less than the mean (neap tides).

Knowledge of tidal rise and fall is of vital interest to the sailor, whose boat normally draws more water than does a powerboat. Even though a boat has a draft (depth from waterline to keel bottom) of four feet, and the chart says five feet is available at a given spot, the boat may run aground during a spring low tide.

For a few minutes after high tide and again after low tide, the current and rise and fall normally take a rest; this period is known as slack water. At all other times rise and fall runs in accordance with a calculable rhythm; one-twelfth of the total the first and sixth hours, two-twelfths at the second and fifth hours, three-twelfths at the third and fourth hours.

Fortunately, tidal current follows channels—the path of least resistance—and is not at its swiftest in most yacht anchorages.

chapter 8

Basic
Sailing Maneuvers

Before actually raising sail, which is the same as starting an engine, it is useful to think about the process of harnessing wind to sail and boat. Even the simple act of sailing from dock or mooring through traffic to open water requires this process.

Whereas expertise may be acquired only through sailing, reading can aid in developing mental pictures which, in turn, can be translated later into physical responses. Lacking any help from the mind, muscles are of little use. Use of the learning aids illustrated in Figure 8-8 will be helpful.

Sailing Toward the Wind

Whether during a sail or simply while leaving the dock for open water, the boat has a definite destination. If the destination is directly upwind, the sailboat is denied a *straight* course to that destination. However, it can get there by a

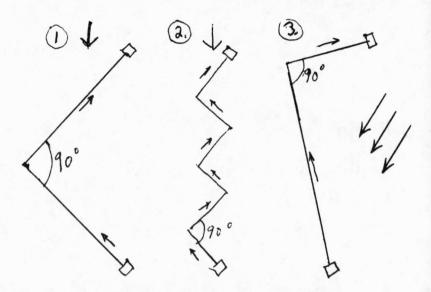

Figure 8-1. Zigzag course needed in sailing to upwind destination.
1. Two tacks, making only one 90-degree turn. 2. Several shorter tacks. 3. One long and one short tack, made possible when the wind is at a slight angle, not directly against the desired course.

zigzag course, each zig and each zag being made at an angle of 45 degrees to the wind (also to the destination in this example). Thus, the course requires a series of two or more 90-degree turns (45 degrees plus 45 degrees).

The process of sailing upwind is variously called "sailing close-hauled," "beating," "sailing on the wind," "sailing upwind," all of which terms are more or less interchangeable. Sailing on a straight course, with no turning, is called sailing "on a tack." Turning from one tack to the other is called "tacking" or sometimes "coming about."

Being denied free access to a full quarter of the horizon,

the sailor expects to spend much more time beating than sailing at any other angle to the wind. This is why experienced sailors place strong emphasis on developing skill in sailing to windward.

Although spray in the face is an occasional factor in beating, the *sensation* of sailing speed is enhanced because of the fact that wind speed and boat speed are added together to yield the resultant stronger apparent wind felt by the sailor. Other assets are an easier sense of exactly where the wind is coming from, and the liveliness of the boat. In sum, the assets outweigh the liabilities.

In beating there are the same two controls used for all points of sailing: rudder and sail control rope.

As noted in Chapter 5, the sail is trimmed quite close to the boat's centerline. One rule of thumb on this is to trim so that the boom, or its extension, aims over the corner of the back of the boat.

Once proper trim has been established, it need be changed only when the boat is steered to a different angle with the wind, or in small boats when the wind strength increases so as to cause excessive heeling, in which case the sheet is loosened ("payed out" or "eased") until the heeling angle tames down. (In small centerboard boats the sailor should keep the control line in his hand, ready to pull in or let out, whereas in larger keel boats this line may safely be cleated down.)

The rudder is guided so as to maintain an optimum angle between sail and wind ("optimum" means that the boat goes with an easy drive as close as possible to the wind and does not heel excessively). With each of the constant wind shifts, the sailor steers his boat to keep that optimum angle. Sailing on a beat is the only time a sailor properly steers a snaky course.

If the boat is steered too close to the wind, the curve of the sail will cause its forward third to edge directly into the wind.

Figure 8-2. Sailing close-hauled.
The arrow indicates wind direction. Note that the boom aims over the corner of the back of the boat.

This action will result in shaking (luffing) caused by the buffeting of the wind now meeting the cloth on both sides. The sailor corrects by steering slightly away from the wind to regain the 45-degree angle; shaking stops immediately. Unfortunately for the beginner, however, there is no luffing to signal when the boat has turned too far away from the wind. Especially in light winds, when the sail has filled and the luffing stops, a novice can turn the boat all the way downwind (an arc of 135 degrees!) with no clear signal from any source. (In fresh breezes, steering too far from the wind with sail trimmed for beating can cause a light centerboard boat to heel excessively and can result in a capsize.)

There are several techniques for re-establishing the optimum angle once lost. One is to steer the boat gradually toward the wind until the sail just begins to luff, then to steer a very few degrees away from the wind—just enough to stop the luffing. Another technique is to fix visually the angle of a weather vane (or masthead fly) or a telltale yarn in the rigging when the boat is known to be sailing at optimum; whenever the masthead fly or telltale wanders from that angle, the course can be changed to return it to the "fix." A third technique is to maintain an angle of the boat to the wave pattern. Under most conditions wave patterns are stable and "readable" for long periods of time.

Actually, maintaining an optimum course close to the wind requires the cultivation of all the senses. Vision has been covered above. Here are tips for using the others:

Feeling: 1) Balance. When the boat luffs, it comes more upright. When it is too far from (or "off") the wind, it heels more.

2) Reduced or added pressure of body against rail or cockpit seat, as the boat comes upright or heels more.

3) Feel of tiller as the water past the rudder increases or reduces pressure.

4) Change of wind pressure on one's skin—face, neck, etc.

Hearing: 1) Change in sounds of water at bow, sides, stern, and bottom of boat.

2) Rigging sounds. When a boat luffs to the extreme, its sail shakes or slaps back and forth near the mast and the sail slides or slugs rattle quite loudly.

Studying the coordination of wind, sail and boat angles by using the learning aids illustrated in Figure 8-8 will show that the farther from the wind a boat sails the longer time will be required to reach an upwind destination. For instance, if the boat is tacked at an angle of 90 degrees to the wind, then is again tacked at this angle, the two courses will be reciprocal (180 degrees). Like the fabled *Flying Dutchman*, the sailor so steering will sail the same track forever. The 90-degree example is used because it is easy to understand. However, by precisely the same token, angles of 50, 60, or 65 degrees from the wind result in delays in direct proportion to their departure from the optimum of about 45 degrees.

Another calculation must be made in order to reach an up-wind destination. It has been shown that tacking toward the wind proceeds by a series of right angle hitches, each bringing the boat closer to the destination. The reader might well ask why not make only two long tacks instead of the several shorter ones shown in Figure 8-1. This is quite possible when there is enough space to sail out to the "lay line," the course on which, by sailing straight, one can reach the target with but one more tack. The only problem with this technique is that wind shifts cause more course changes on a long hitch (leg) than on a short one, and the sailor may end up making a number of shorter tacks to advantage.

The reader might also ask how to tell when to tack so as to reach the destination without further tacking. The answer is simple. Since most boats beat at 45 degrees to the wind, the turn from one tack to the other is a right angle, and one may tack with reasonable assurance of fetching (laying) an object bearing at right angles, barring the drift caused by tide and by the sidewise slipping of the boat away from the wind (to leeward). All sailboats make some slippage (leeway); so a few degrees past the right angle is usually good insurance.

It is good practice to keep one's weight on the windward (high) side of the boat except on days with light winds, when weight sometimes helps on the downwind (low) side. When the boat tips, weight on the high side curtails tipping. A heeling (tipping) angle of fifteen to twenty degrees is optimum in most boats, and they are designed to sail faster at that angle. An angle greater than twenty degrees should be avoided by weight movement, easing the sheet, or pointing slightly "higher" (toward the wind), perhaps even allowing the sail to luff a little. Light dinghies often sail fastest upwind at a heeling angle of five to ten degrees.

When one must beat through an anchorage or other traffic area, the target, or destination, will be a space between two obstacles. Perhaps the area in question has limited space and one can sail only a short distance on each tack. Under such circumstances several tacks will be required, and each will demand planning ahead so as to lay the next course through open water and not through other boats, moorings, mooring lines, or dinghy tethers (painters).

To sum up, when you are beating, always remember the following pointers:

1) Sail as close to the wind as possible without luffing.
2) Guard against heeling too much, especially in small centerboard boats.
3) Plan the zigzag headings to reach the destination with the smallest number of tacks.
4) In crowded quarters be careful to plan ahead for each tack so as to sail toward open water, not obstructions.

Tacking

In the preceding topic, the act of tacking was mentioned but not explained in detail.

To tack is to change the wind from one side of the boat to the other by steering the boat into the wind, past it, and over to its other side. For example, if the wind is from the right side, the sailor must turn the boat to the right until the wind comes from the left side. Assuming he wishes to sail on, the wind must come from this new side at an angle sufficient to drive the boat (45 degrees or more).

To be most efficient, the act of tacking should be smooth but definite. To tack smoothly requires a constant-radius turn made with no indecision and a radius more than minimal. Pushing the rudder far over and very quickly makes the rudder more of a brake than a steering device. On the other hand, moving the rudder very gingerly results in a turn with a radius so long that the boat's momentum can be lost before the turn is complete. Remember that throughout a routine

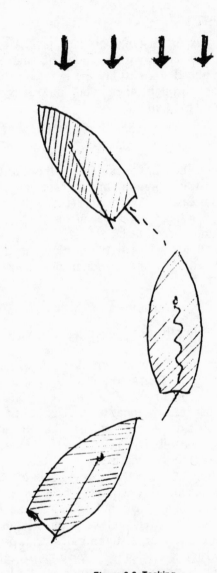

Figure 8-3. Tacking.
To tack, turn boat into and past the wind, indicated by arrows. Straighten boat
on new tack when wind comes from new side.

tacking procedure, the boat is without sail power and hence will quite quickly lose forward motion. *Maintaining boat speed is essential.*

Tacking is executed by moving the tiller toward the sail, or with a wheel by turning the wheel away from the sail. For beginners it is usually important to face forward during the entire maneuver. Later one can look back to observe his wake and sheet trim.

Sailing with the Wind from the Side

When the wind is from a point farther from the bow than the 45 degrees optimum for beating, and in fact from any angle between that point and any other point ahead of the stern, the boat is said to be "reaching." Since reaching covers an arc of about 125-130 degrees, sailors divide the category into three segments for more specific description. With the wind between 45 degrees and 90 degrees from the bow, the boat is on a "close reach." When the wind is precisely at 90 degrees, or directly "abeam," the point is a "beam reach." With the wind between 90 degrees and 170-175 degrees, it becomes a "broad reach." To make it easy to remember: a *close* reach is the reach in which the boat is sailing *closest* to the wind; a *beam* reach is the reach in which the wind is *abeam*; and a *broad* reach is the reach in which the wind is at a wide, or *broad*, angle to the bow of the boat.

On reaches the boat may be sailed on a consistently straight course. Compensation for wind shifts is made by changing sail angle, "trimming," or "easing off" the sail's control line. On all points of sailing except beating the shortest distance to the destination for most sailboats is a straight line (except when currents cause crabbing).

Since all reaches are at angles different from that in beating, and since each category of reach is at an angle different from that of other reaches, the sail must be trimmed differently for each. Failing to change sail angle by easing out the control line when turning *away from* the wind lowers speed. In fresh breezes, this omission invites high angles of heel and, for centerboard boats, even capsizing. Failure to adjust when turning *toward* the wind lowers speed and causes luffing.

To learn how to readjust sail angle when changing course from a beat to a reach or from a close reach to a beam or broad reach, proceed as follows: Select a point—compass course, house on shore, a clump of trees, etc.—which will put the boat on the desired point of sailing. Let the sail out until it starts to shake a little near the mast and above its midpoint. Then trim it in until the shaking (luffing) stops.

Once on a reaching course, compensation for wind shifts is by sheet changes only. While trimming, however, it is most important to maintain a very straight course to the objective point, because sail changes are nullified by course changes.

Wind shifts can be readily seen by watching vanes, tell-tales, shore smoke, cigarette smoke, etc.—or, best of all, felt by the skin. If the wind shifts toward the bow, the sail must be pulled in. If the shift is toward the stern, the sail should be let out. Shifts to the bow will be easier to observe, since these will be accompanied and signaled by luffing of the sail(s).

In light winds efficient alterations in sail trim or sail angle may be quite difficult for the inexperienced sailor to make, since the signs are low key and the sheet and tiller actions are sluggish. However, under light air conditions these adjustments are of primary importance for maintaining maximum boat speed. In all winds the boat will sail more efficiently when trimmed to all wind shifts.

In trimming for a beam reach, the sail should be let out about one-third to one-half of its potential arc just as the boat is turned to one-third to one-half of its turning arc from close-hauled to wind behind. Start with this and thereafter

Figure 8-4. Sailing on a beam reach.
Wind direction is shown by arrow. Note that the sail is let out about one-third to one-half of its potential arc.

make the proportionate sail trim/boat angle adjustments for other reaches.

The act of tacking is not restricted to beating. It can be executed from any point of sailing. By definition, it will be recalled, tacking is simply the act of changing the wind from one side to the other. Of course, when coming about from one very broad reach to the other, the arc of turn can be as much as 350 degrees. Throughout that arc, the boat is moving with diminishing wind power, and may lose momentum (way). Loss of way can mean total stopping if such loss should occur before the wind reaches the new side and starts driving. This magnitude of arc can be executed easily in heavy keel boats, but in lighter boats it very often will not work. Higher winds bring higher speeds but also higher waves, and each wave during tacking hammers away a bit of the speed—with the result that long tacking maneuvers in higher winds can easily be doomed to failure, where possibly those tried in light winds will succeed. Such loss of way, and speed, can be avoided by changing sail trim to match the changing angle of wind to boat. That is, as the boat approaches the wind during the turn, the sailor should pull the sail in; then, as the boat leaves the wind on its path to the next course (broad reach, beam reach, or other), he should ease the sail out to the trim proper for that new course.

Sailing with the Wind Behind

Sailors have several terms to describe this point of sailing: "sailing with the wind," "sailing free," "running," "running free," "sailing with the wind aft" ("aft" is sailor-ese for behind), "sailing before the wind," "sailing downwind," and "sailing with a following wind."

By any name, sailing with the wind behind is at once simple and challenging. It is simple because it requires little sail trim (at least to the nonracer) as long as the wind continues to blow from the side opposite the boom. The sail is eased out as far as it can go (usually till the boom is touching

Figure 8-5. Running.
The sail is eased out as far as it can go. Arrow indicates wind direction.

or very near the shrouds). The fact that one is trying to run away from the wind results in the sense of greatly reduced wind velocity and attendant freedom from spray and other concomitants of beating. However, it is challenging because of the constant need to guard against allowing the wind to shift *toward* the sail, where it can sneak around behind it. If unanticipated, this will result in an unfettered swing of the boom from about ninety degrees on one side to the same place on the other side. In so doing, the boom develops a formidable amount of energy which can wreak havoc against the rigging—or against the sailor's head. These unpleasant results can be avoided by paying constant attention to wind direction. When the wind is seen to sneak over to the side the sail is on, head the boat enough away from the boom side to bring the wind back where it belongs. Actually, the signals are plentiful when one is watching for them. First, the wind change is felt on the back of the neck. Telltales and masthead fly show it. The boom shows it by attempting to lift in a restive manner. At any time during these signalings, unpleasant results can be avoided by turning the boat *away from the sail.*

As in reaching, sailing downwind is normally a straight line, so long as the wind does not shift *toward* the sail. Sheet trim alone should adjust for any shift the wind makes *away from* the sail.

Many boats are equipped with a boom vang (see Fig. 8-6). The vang is a wire or system of ropes which run diagonally from a point two to three feet out from the mast on the boom downwards and forward at about a 45-degree angle towards the foot of the mast or the floorboards of the boat near the base of the mast. Its purpose is to keep the boom from rising and from swinging across when you don't want it to. A vang provides safety by minimizing the possibility of capsizing when running before the wind and maintains sail horsepower during reaching and running by keeping the sail from twisting.

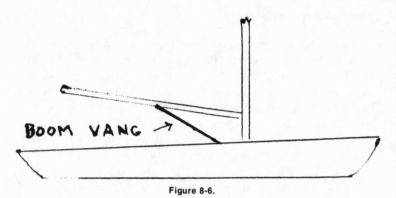

Figure 8-6.

Tacking may be executed from a run just as outlined for a broad reach. However, having even farther to turn, few small boats will have weight enough (hence, speed enough) to complete the tack without trimming the sheet in while turning toward the wind, then easing it out while turning away from the wind onto the new course. This next course can be a beat, a reach, or another run; and for each the sail is, of course, adjusted to suit.

When turning from any other course to a run, the sailor may feel that the wind has dropped and the weather has changed. In fact, the wind has dropped, but only on the boat. This is because, when running, the boat's speed is subtracted from wind speed; the boat is attempting to run away from the wind. As soon as a turn is made back toward the wind, the apparent velocity will once again increase. This apparent change in wind velocity is demonstrated in reverse when beating, a course which makes the wind seem stronger than it is.

The Jibe and When to Use It

A jibe is the inverse of tacking. Whereas the latter consists of changing the wind from one side to the other by turning the boat away from the sail, a jibe changes the wind from one side to the other by turning the boat toward the sail. *A jibe can be executed only when the boat is pointing downwind,* whether it is sailing on that point or is merely in the process of turning from another course. A jibe can be executed *from* any point of sailing, and *to* any point of sailing. When a jibe is planned, it is a safe and simple maneuver. Only when unanticipated—caused by inadvertence or carelessness—is there potential danger or damage in a jibe.

To jibe, move the tiller *away from* the sail, and a wheel *toward* it.

A jibe is used when it will bring the boat to the desired course more simply and quickly than tacking will. As this chapter has shown, tacking from one run or reach to another is unnecessarily time-consuming and even problematical regarding maintenance of boat speed. Conversely, a jibe from one reach or run to another can be made quickly in a relatively short arc and with wind power throughout. By the same token, tacking from close-hauled to another course on the opposite tack will be quick and will lose wind power for only a short time because of the minimal arc of turn.

The technique of jibing is quite simple, but it does require smooth coordination between tiller and sheet. Jibing from a run, first pull the sheet all the way in; then steer the boat toward the sail only far enough to get the wind on the sail's other side. The boom will then come across the boat, its movement gentle since it has no distance in which to build momentum. After the boom crosses the boat, ease the sheet out until the sail is at the angle suited to the new course. In fresh breezes, this letting out might be better described as "letting go," since wind pressure will start the boom moving at a speed high enough to blister unaccustomed hands.

After the basics of jibing are mastered, you may wish to consider refinements that give more control for medium and light air jibing. Face either forward or back. Steer to the jibe point. Put the tiller between your knees. Seize several or all

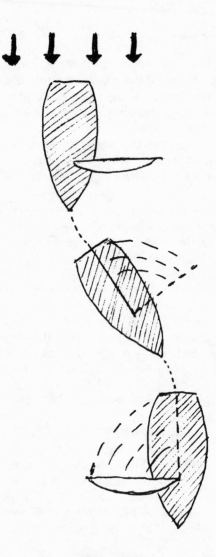

Figure 8-7. Jibing.
In jibing, wind must be from behind the boat, as shown by arrows. To jibe, pull the sail in, let the wind come from the new side, and let the sail out. A jibe is facilitated by turning the boat slightly toward the sail as the sail is pulled in, then resuming course after sail is out on new side.

"parts" of the mainsheet together in one hand. Using one or two hands, pull it (and the boom) to the midline of the boat. As the wind takes the sail at the centerline, let it out to the new side and recapture the tiller with either hand. Adjust the tiller to the new course.

How and where the mainsheet leads (and thus how and where it is easiest to grab two or more parts at the same time) may determine whether it is easier to face backward during such a jibe. Of course, the helmsman is normally standing throughout this maneuver and may have to duck or squat when the boom swings by.

Jibing from a reach or a beat, on light centerboard boats ease out the sail to its run position prior to arriving at the run course (sheet and turn should be coordinated). Then hold the run course while you pull the sail in as described above. Finally, make the turn toward the sail and let the sheet go out. Keel boats with ample rudders will be able to jibe from any point without letting the sail out initially. However, in any boat the sail must come in just before, and be let out just after, the actual act of jibing.

The above-outlined jibing technique is suited to almost all sailboats above 12-14 feet in length, and it is stressed simply because it is the "classic" jibing technique. However, jibing is done somewhat differently in light, unstable boats such as Sunfish, Sailfish, other board boats, and the light, small sailing dinghies.

As in any other boat, jibing these small boats in very light airs requires little technique, since few hazards are involved. However, when the breeze picks up, these boats are jibed as follows: From any point of sailing, simply turn rather sharply into a jibe (boat toward sail). Do not pull sail in before the jibe and then out afterwards. Simply let the sail come over—and duck! During and immediately after the jibe, adjust the sail trim to the next course.

This technique is obviously very simple and the reader

may wonder why it is not recommended for larger boats. To answer briefly: on a small, light boat the boom/sail combination has a very small weight (momentum), the sheeting is simple, and there is no gear, such as permanent or running backstays, shrouds, etc., for the boom to break.

In two-man boats and in light winds, there is a technique whereby the crew can provide help in moving the boom against wind pressure to the middle of the boat. At the command, "Stand by to jibe," the crew faces partly sidewise in the boat and places his forward hand against the rail or something solid near the rail, and his aft hand (palm up) on the boom. At the command, "Jibing," he pushes with his forward hand and pulls the boom toward the centerline with his other hand. This procedure permits the crew to apply a lot of shoulder and back power without much exertion. With practice it leads to a smooth jibe executed jointly by crew and skipper. If the boat is on the port tack (boom on right side) before the jibe onto the starboard tack, the crew's left hand is forward and on the boat, and his right hand is on the boom, ready to pull on command. The crew is in a squatting position for this maneuver. In heavy winds the crew can be more useful by keeping his weight on the high side and by helping handle the sheet.

Learning Aids

Using the learning aids illustrated in Figure 8-8 will help the reader fix firmly in his mind the relationships between sail to boat, boat to wind, and sail to wind in all points of sailing. The learning aids consist of a chart of the complete sailing horizon and silhouettes representing the boat and boom and sail. In the chart of the sailing horizon, the arrows at the top represent the wind direction. The chart shows those segments of the sailing pie constituting no-man's-land, sailing close-

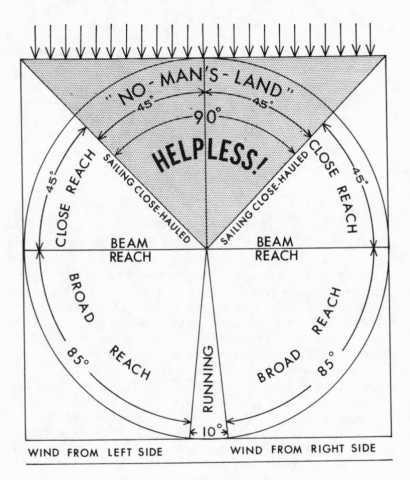

Figure 8-8. Learning aids.

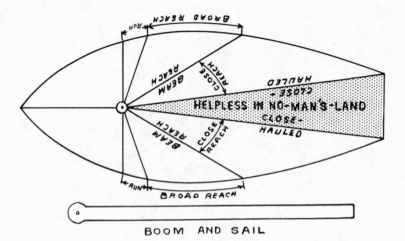

BOOM AND SAIL

Figure 8-8. Learning aids (cont.).

hauled (or beating), a close reach with the wind coming both from the left and the right, a broad reach with the wind coming from the left and the right, and running.

To use these learning aids, copy them on tracing paper, transfer the copies via carbon paper to a shirt board or other bit of cardboard, and cut them out. Hinge the boom and sail onto the boat with a pin. Place the boat on the chart facing in any direction (except, of course, into no-man's-land) with its center over the chart's center. If you have aimed the boat into an area marked "CLOSE REACH," place boom and sail within one of the boat's areas marked "CLOSE REACH." Boom and sail must be on the side of the boat away from the wind. If the boat points to the segment marked "RUNNING," place the boom on the line marked "RUN." If you have aimed the boat into a section labeled "BROAD REACH," put the boom within an area of the boat marked "BROAD REACH." If the boat points into "no-man's-land," the boom must, of course, also be located in "no-man's-land," and it will be helpless.

chapter 9

Practice Exercises in Boat Control

Having made a start at understanding sailing maneuvers, the sailor can plan practice sessions to put what he has learned to use. Each of the maneuvers outlined in Chapter 8 is useful in everyday sailing, and the skills acquired in coordinating one with the other are most rewarding.

Repeat each exercise recommended until doing it accurately becomes easy in light winds and the freedom of open water. Later, practice the same exercises in and around traffic and in fresher breezes.

Selecting a Good Practice Area

The best area for practicing will be a half-mile or more square, free of shoals and other hazards, reasonably free from traffic, and far enough from high ground or buildings to permit the wind to reach full strength. Try to select such an area from the chart before leaving on a sail. The first practice session will prove whether your choice was a good one.

Testing Boat Responses

Anyone sailing a boat to which he is unaccustomed needs to find out how it will respond to his control. You can test all a boat's characteristics, both normal and otherwise, by performing the following experiments:

Momentum. From full sailing speed head the boat into the wind and observe the distance its momentum will take it before it stops. This distance is an extremely important factor in many maneuvers, especially landings.

Turning Radius. Part of every boat's individual personality is its turning radius. This radius is a function of hull design, rudder size and location, and boat weight. A long, heavy boat with conventional keel and rudder hinged to that keel, will take far more distance to turn than will a short, light boat with a rudder far back of the keel or centerboard.

To observe a boat's characteristic turning radius, hold the tiller about halfway over, just as in the start of a smooth tacking maneuver. Moving the tiller more tends to stop headway, while moving it less yields an uncharacteristic radius. To obtain a mental picture of the radius, at the end of the turn glance back at the boat's wake, which remains for a few seconds as a graphic chart of the boat's passage. The wake should form a fair curve, not a square. Test your boat further by making turns of varying radii and observing their effects on boat speed.

Controlling Heel. Experiment with sail trim while sailing on a beat, a close reach, and a beam reach. Start by trimming for efficiency; then pull the sheet in more. Observe the change in heel (none if the wind is very light, but considerable in fresh winds). Again, watch the result of easing the

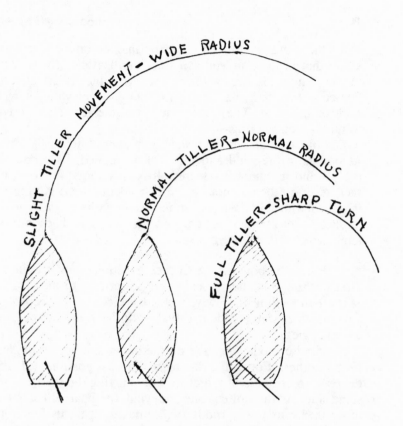

Figure 9-1. Turning radii.

sheet out. Next, experiment with weight shifting—first to leeward, then to the "high" side (as far to windward as possible). Use these weight shifts on the various points of sailing.

In experimenting with heeling the boat to windward and to leeward, start conservatively and grow somewhat bolder. In small boats you may discover, while heeling to windward, that the "feel," or "helm," has gone out of the tiller, that if you actually release the tiller, the boat may head away from the wind. A little more experimentation will demon-strate that in light air you can steer the boat effectively with "body English" and without touching the tiller at all. Someday this skill may come in handy. Meanwhile, it will build confidence. The larger the boat, the less effect crew weight has on steering.

Getting in and out of Irons. A boat is "in irons" when its bow is to the wind and the boat is stopped. Its rudder is useless and it cannot be steered. It is easy to get in irons; in fact, testing a boat's momentum just about *means* getting in irons. Getting out is also simple because there are several applicable techniques designed to put the boat back on an angle which will engage the wind.

1) Force the bow over with rudder action. This is done by first pushing the tiller quickly and powerfully to the desired side, then pulling it slowly back to the centerline; repeated several times, these rudder thrusts will drive the bow to the useful angle.

2) Stand up; put one hand on the boom and hold the tiller in the other. Force the boom as far as possible (20-25 degrees) to one side of the centerline, moving the tiller to the same side. As the sail engages the wind, the boat will start to move backwards. The rudder will quickly regain its function as the boat begins to move backwards, and the boat will turn towards the boom. As soon as the boat has turned suf-ficiently, pull the tiller to the side opposite the boom with vigor, trim the mainsail, and you are under way again.

A lazy man's technique for getting out of irons is to do nothing and wait until the boat is blown sideways so that the sail will engage the wind. However, in some small boats in fresh breezes this may not work.

If a jib is in use (see Chapter 13), getting out of irons is simplicity itself. Using one of the two jib sheets, pull the back corner of the jib as far away from the centerline as possible.

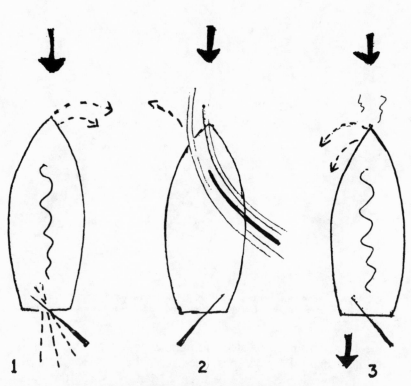

Figure 9-2. Three ways to get out of irons.
1. By forceful movements of tiller, boat's front end can be forced to turn enough for sail to engage wind. 2. By manually forcing sail out toward wind, the boat's front end will be forced in direction away from sail. 3. If the boat is allowed to drift backward with the wind, the boat's front end will move in the direction in which you push the tiller. This is a reversal of normal frontward technique.

The angle the jib thus makes will engage the wind near the bow and will thus force the boat to turn onto a sailing course. As soon as possible, trim the jib normally by its lee sheet.

Helm. "Helm" is the word for any lever used for steering. It is also the word used to describe the tendency inherent in a sailboat to take over and steer itself. If a boat tends to turn toward the wind, it is said to have "weather (windward) helm." If it turns naturally away from the wind, it has "lee helm." If neither tendency is present, and

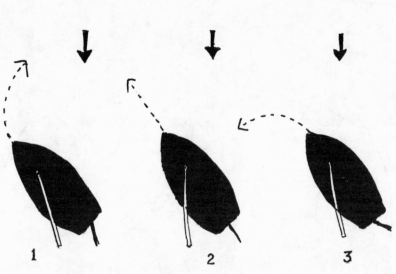

Figure 9-3. Helm.
1. Weather helm turns boat toward wind. 2. Neutral helm does not affect steering.
3. Lee helm turns boat away from wind. (Note that rudder must be used to counteract
helm force.)

the boat continues to steer straight ahead when the tiller is relinquished, the boat has "neutral helm." A lee helm is an inconvenience, possibly even a danger, since the final result of giving a lee helm free play is a jibe. Neutral helm incurs the least amount of friction (drag) to impede speed, because it does not require use of the rudder to keep a straight course (any movement of the rudder from a straight, streamlined position means dragging that much rudder through the water at a resisting angle). However, weather helm, though adding drag, is designed into most boats and is almost always present in boats sailed with mainsail alone. It is a safety measure for sailors lacking considerable experience, since under its guidance the boat will turn toward the wind, where the worst result will be merely stopping.

In testing a boat's responses, the presence of helm can be discovered very quickly: simply take hands off the tiller and see which way the boat turns.

Because of the nature of the gearing which links a wheel to the rudder, the helm on most boats with wheels does not take over when the wheel is left to its own devices.

Influence of Crew Weight. While sailing normally, try moving your weight from side to side and from front to back, in order to observe the boat's reaction. Many well-balanced boats can be steered by a relatively slight relocation of weight. For instance, when the bow is forced further into the water by changing the boat's trim, the effects of helm are diminished. Inversely, when weight forces the stern down abnormally, helm is increased. Similar effects are possible with lateral weight shifts.

Most boats of thirty feet and under perform and balance best if the weight of crew and helmsman is concentrated at about the midpoint of the boat—that is, halfway from the point at which the boat cleaves the water in the bow to the point where the boat's hull comes out of the water aft towards the stern. This concentration of weight requires the people aboard to sit comfortably but fairly close to one another, about two to three inches apart. As mentioned in Chapter 7, the helmsman should be forward of the arc made by the tip of the tiller. This puts him away from the "novice's corner" (way back in the cockpit) and into the middle third of the cockpit at least.

Sailing "by the Lee." This phrase describes the situation which arises when the boat is sailing downwind and the wind moves over to the side the sail is on. In sailing downwind there is actually no "weather" or "lee" side, but in practice the side the sail is on is always the "lee" side and the other side is "weather." Obviously, when the wind is on the same side as the sail, the latter will be blown across the boat; hence the jibe.

In testing a new boat's reactions, it is extremely useful to experiment with sailing by the lee. Try it with the sail all the way out, halfway in, and in a beating position. Note how

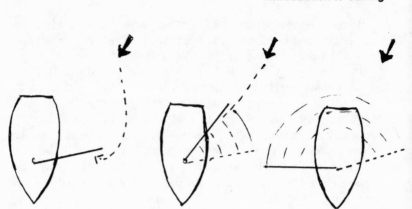

Figure 9-4. Sailing by the lee.
When the wind works around behind the sail as the boat is sailing downwind,
it can blow the boom and sail across the boat with great force. You are by the lee
when the wind is coming (even at a very slight angle) from the sail side.

much more quickly a given angle of wind will drive the boom
over when the sail is in, and how relatively slowly when the
sail is way out. Observe the signals from the sail, the boom,
and the telltales just before the jibe starts. When these signals
first start, note how simply they can be stopped by steering
quickly away from the sail. The more one can learn about the
boat's characteristics when sailing by the lee, the more simply will jibes be executed in stronger breezes.

The experienced sailor will know when he is sailing by the
lee by the feel of the wind on his face or neck, or perhaps by
a difference in the wind sound in one ear as compared with
the other. However, a sure-fire signal for all sailors is a good
masthead fly. Its height over the water and freedom from obstruction to wind approach give it an advantage over other
devices. Jim Merrill of Merrill Sails, Delanco, New Jersey,
sells an excellent masthead fly.

Headreaching

Much can be learned by combining two or more of the boat-handling experiments. For instance, momentum and getting in irons combine to make "headreaching," which is the planned use of momentum while facing the wind. Headreaching is used for making landings, for man-overboard rescues, even by experts for stretching a tack to round the last few feet of a mooring line when beating through an anchorage. Headreaching stops just short of actually getting in irons, and can therefore be considered a controlled maneuver.

"Automatic Pilot"

Sailors often find it helpful to use weather helm and sail trim together. With the sheet let out to a beam reach setting, relinquishing the tiller will cause the boat to steer toward the wind far enough to slow it down considerably, but because of the freed sheet the boat will not come about or get in irons. This situation is called "lying to." However, for the

Figure 9-5. Lying to.
Release tiller, let sail out at least halfway, and relax. The boat will take over from you and for you.

learning sailor it becomes a most useful "automatic pilot." The boat will stay on this automatic pilot, moving very slowly, for a very long time, thus granting the sailor much time to take care of business away from the tiller.

"Lying to" is a very fine and important confidence builder. There are two points to remember: (1) Don't do this when sailing downwind, because the result can quite easily be an unexpected jibe. (2) Do not fail to release the mainsail to a position at least halfway out. If retained in a close-hauled trim, the boat will tend to tack each time it points toward the wind; and if a jib is in use, the boat can continue into a complete circle with attendant jibing.

Sailing Close-hauled

The reader will find it helpful, in practicing this exercise, to use the learning aids illustrated in Figure 8-8. Proceed as follows: (1) Trim the sheet so that the boom, or its extension, is located over one corner of the stern. (2) Steer toward the wind until the sail's forward edge begins to shake. (3) Steer away from the wind just enough to stop the shake. (4) Keep the boat at this angle to the wind, making any turns needed to do so but not changing sheet trim unless a heavy gust causes excessive heeling. (5) Maintain this course "on the wind" for a few minutes.

Tacking from a Close-hauled Angle. (1) Without changing sheet trim, turn the boat with a firm motion, putting the tiller approximately halfway over. (2) As the boat loses speed in the turn, move the tiller further over. (3) Just *before* the new course is gained, bring the tiller back to centerline with a slow but definite motion. (Failure to anticipate in turning will result in oversteering.) If the boat has considerable weather helm (many do with mainsail alone), the tiller will need to be past the centerline on the new weather side in order to keep a straight course. (4) *Before any turn, look toward the next course to be sure no traffic will be on it.* (5) Use your weight to keep the boat in trim, which means heeling no more than 15-20 degrees. Move weight to the new weather side only after the sail has moved across, not before. Shifting weight too early can aggravate tipping. (6) After tacking, find the optimum course by once again steering toward the wind to get the sail shaking, then steering slightly away for speed.

Jibing from a Close-hauled Angle. (1) Coordinate the sheet and tiller so that the sail goes out as far as it can go while the boat turns to a downwind course. (2) Hold the downwind course while the sheet is pulled back in all the way to minimize the arc of the boom when the wind gets behind it. (3) Turn the boat further toward the sail. (4) Wait for the boat to jibe. (5) Steer to the new course. (6) Let out the sail rather quickly to whatever angle is required for the new course.

Practice jibes from close-hauled to close-hauled, from close-hauled to reach, and from close-hauled to run.

Reaching

(1) Find a convenient point to steer for. (2) Trim the sheet efficiently for that course. (3) Maintain the course strictly, compensating for wind shifts by trimming the sail in or out. (4) If the sail shakes, it is out too far. (5) Pull it in until the shaking just stops. (6) If in doubt about trim, let the sail out until the shake starts, then pull it back.

Tacking from a Reach. (1) Start with the tiller halfway over. (2) Coordinate the sail with the turn by pulling it in; the sail should be in close-hauled location when the boat has turned to the close-hauled angle. (3) As the boat turns further into no-man's-land where speed will diminish, move the tiller further over as in coming about from close-hauled. (4) As the new tack begins, bring the tiller back to halfway and continue the turn until the desired course is reached.

Practice tacking from close, beam, and broad reaches, to close-hauled, reaching, and running courses.

Jibing from a Reach. Proceed precisely as outlined for jibing from close-hauled. Practice jibes from close, beam, and broad reaches to all other points of sailing.

Weight is very important on close reaches to counteract heeling, and on broad reaches mainly to help steering.

Running

(1) Trim the sheet so that the boom is out as far as it will go without seriously chafing on the shrouds. (2) Find a convenient point and steer on a straight course for it. (3) If the wind moves away from the sail, pull the sheet in; if it moves toward the sail, steer the boat away from the sail until the wind is again directly behind.

Tacking from a Run. Proceed just as in reaching to all points of sailing.

Jibing while Running. Holding carefully to the course selected, pull the sail all the way in. Proceed from there just as in jibing from close-hauled. Practice jibing to reaches and close-hauled courses.

Weight is used, as in all other points of sailing, for trim; but in running, the heel problem is normally absent. In light boats weight is best located farther back than on reaches or beats.

Practice Landings

If a buoy, or any anchored float, is available, use that. Or, toss over a life jacket or other floating object. Figure 9-6 shows that in simplest terms a landing pattern consists of a base leg and a final approach leg.

Since heading into the wind until the boat stops is the only undramatic method of stopping a sailboat, the proper loca-

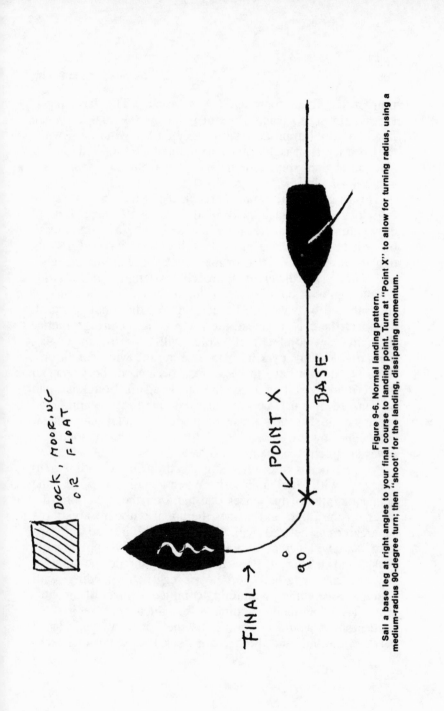

DOCK, MOOR, OR FLOAT

POINT X

FINAL →

90°

BASE

Figure 9-6. Normal landing pattern.

Sail a base leg at right angles to your final course to landing point. Turn at "Point X" to allow for turning radius, using a medium-radius 90-degree turn; then "shoot" for the landing, dissipating momentum.

tion of the final approach leg is crucial. The base leg is located simply to reach a useful point on the final approach line. The final approach is precisely on the wind axis, while the base leg is at right angles to the axis on either side of it. The sailor can approach the base leg from any point—upwind, downwind, etc.

The length of the final approach leg is also crucial, since too long a distance will find the boat fresh out of momentum—landing short; while too short a distance will bring it to the mooring or dock with excessive speed, risking damage to boat and dock, or inability to hold on for the landing. There is a different approach leg length for each different combination of wind velocity, wave height, current strength and boat weight. In learning to judge final approach distance, there is no substitute for practice. During practice the sailor develops a "feel" which will be useful in judging the variables for any kind of boat, sea, and wind conditions. Landings do not have to be perfect, because a short one can be rectified by sailing away and trying again. Long ones can be handled by muscle power, or by sailing to try again. Good landings satisfy one's sense of pride and allay subsequent comments by the "rocking chair fleet," which somehow always happens to see one's mistakes.

A good means of diminishing speed during a landing is to "brake" with the mainsail. When head to wind, the helmsman stands up, places one hand on the boom and the other on the tiller, and pushes the boom outboard about 15-30 degrees. The sail will "come aback" instead of flapping, and will act as a brake. By alternately applying the brake and letting it flap, the skipper should be able to produce an "eggshell" or near "eggshell" landing with little practice while maintaining complete control of the situation. (An "eggshell" landing is so called because it is so gentle that it would not crack the shell of a raw egg placed between the hull and the buoy or dock.) As with other tech-

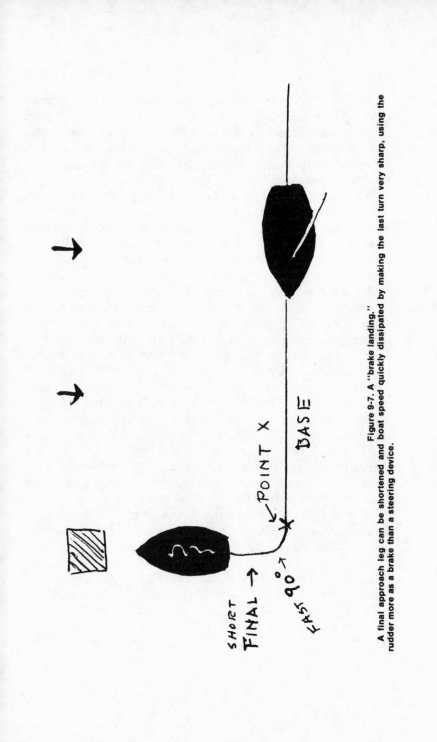

Figure 9-7. A "brake landing."

A final approach leg can be shortened and boat speed quickly dissipated by making the last turn very sharp, using the rudder more as a brake than a steering device.

niques of making a landing, the beginner should practice braking with the mainsail on a mooring or small buoy until he feels he has gotten the hang of it. The braking stance (standing up) is the same as used for "backing down" with "reverse" sailpower in order to get out of irons quickly, a procedure discussed earlier in this chapter.

Whether approaching a practice landing from reach, run, or beat, the beginner should select an invisible point in the water, downwind of the floating object but sufficiently toward him to allow for turning radius and at a distance judged effective for the conditions on the day in question— "Point X."

From a Beat. Sail, on as many tacks as are required, to arrive at Point X. Just prior to crossing that point, turn toward the mark (turning radius must be allowed for). Use an easy, not too precipitate turn. Aim at the mark and wait. The landing is *adequate* if the boat gets to the mark at a speed considered controllable by muscle power. It is *excellent* if the boat makes an "eggshell" landing by sidling up to the mark and halting there a few inches from it with no way on. Repeat this procedure until you can make at least an adequate landing.

From a Reach. Aim directly at Point X, and proceed thereafter as from a beat. However, if the approach is by broad reach, trim the sail in to a beam reach position in order to sail the right-angle base leg efficiently.

From a Run. Sail downwind to the normal base leg. Turn 90 degrees onto the base leg, trimming the sail in as the boat turns. Proceed thereafter as in reaching.

There are two additional techniques for landing which are useful under crowded anchorage conditions. One might be called the braking landing, since it varies from the above-outlined classic technique only by a sudden, full-over use of the tiller. When pushed over quickly and completely, the

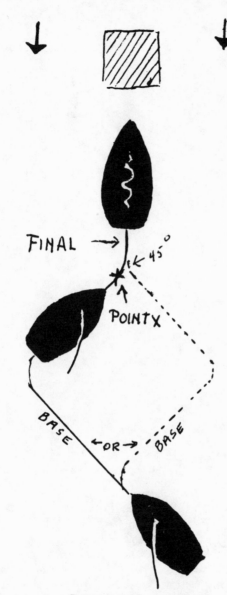

Figure 9-8. Landing from a beat.
Whenever you approach the landing on a zigzag, close-hauled course, the base leg is either a 45-degree zig or zag, and the final approach leg comes out of a 45-degree turn.

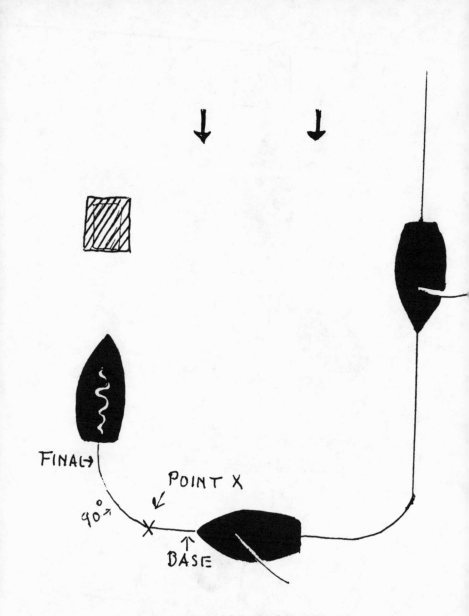

Figure 9-9. Landing from a run.
When approaching landing downwind, merely sail *down* to the normal base leg; then proceed as in Figure 9-6.

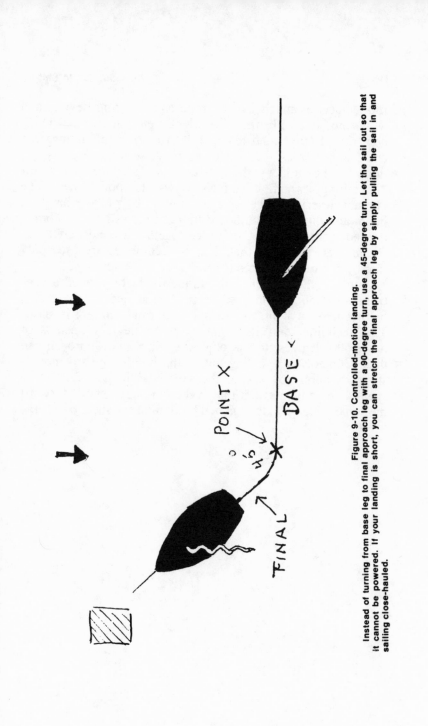

POINT X

BASE

FINAL

Figure 9-10. Controlled-motion landing.

Instead of turning from base leg to final approach leg with a 90-degree turn, use a 45-degree turn. Let the sail out so that it cannot be powered. If your landing is short, you can stretch the final approach leg by simply pulling the sail in and sailing close-hauled.

rudder acts as much like a brake as a steering device; and while the boat will turn, it will be decelerating at a remarkable rate. From broad reaches and runs, brake landings can cut distance by 50 percent or more. A series of braking actions by the rudder—right, left, right—produces a form of "fishtailing" which effectively slows the boat down. The already described technique of braking by placing hand on boom and pushing it outboard to make the sail act as a brake is even more effective. Both used together are most effective. Remember, however, that braking techniques are used only in crowded quarters or to control a too fast approach.

Another close-quarters technique might be termed a controlled-motion landing, since it is designed to avoid the helplessness of being in irons if a normal landing is short. This technique has its Point X at 45 degrees, instead of nearly 90 degrees, to the objective. The final approach can thus be made at a sailing angle, the boat's forward motion stopped merely by letting the sail out, "in neutral," so to speak. The advantage is that if the landing is short, forward motion can be quickly regained by pulling the sheet back in.

chapter 10

Preparing for a Sail

Second in importance only to knowledge of wind direction, planning ahead is required for every move in sailing. Although the expert plans almost without awareness, those new to sailing must plan deliberately.

It requires planning to sail the boat away from the mooring and out through the anchored and moving boats nearby. Still more planning is needed to execute practice maneuvers, and return to the mooring or dock.

Prior planning frees the sailor to concentrate on execution and hence is well worth considerable effort. For instance, practice planning the moves incident to going sailing each time you pass a harbor or anchorage. Plan what would be required under various wind directions or conditions. With familiarization, you can practice this exercise in an easy chair by using mental images of locale and action planned.

On a sailing day, planning while lying quietly at anchor is far superior to attempting to plan after the sail is up and active, or after the boat is untied and underway.

Planning requires understanding of what is to be done. One must make decisions on what sails to raise and what items of hardware to use.

This chapter touches on these subjects and others related to them. To increase intelligibility, nautical terms will be introduced whenever the equivalent layman's language would be too complicated. Once used, these nautical terms will thenceforth be used exclusively.

What to Wear

Sailors are informal in dress. Whatever is comfortable and adequate to the temperature is perfectly acceptable. It is well to plan for temperatures several degrees below those ashore, since even on the hottest days open water brings the temperature down. Never, when the wind is blowing even moderately, is it superfluous or "chicken" to have a sweater with you. Likewise, *do* wear a life jacket while afloat any time you feel safer doing so. Olympic contenders in the yachting events, even gold medallists, wear them. Why shouldn't you?

It is also advisable to bring "foul weather gear" on all sailing days. This means two-piece waterproof suits, available from all boat supply stores in a wide range of prices. It is a wryly useful adage that what you don't bring you'll need.

Men with receding hairlines or worse should bring headgear of some kind. Long-visored caps shade the eyes from the sun.

Persons whose eyes are sensitive to sunlight should wear good-quality sunglasses. Cheap plastic ones get scratched and can make vision worse rather than better.

Those with sensitive skin should protect themselves with a filter lotion at all times. Everyone should have such a lotion with him. The sun's actinic rays are doubly strong on a boat, since they are reflected from the water as well as radiated direct. Even on overcast days the burning effect is considerable, and even the best tan can get a burn on top.

Perhaps the most important article of attire is good, nonskid shoes. Leather soles are, of course, out of the question, since they not only scratch paint and varnish but are quite slippery. Plain rubber soles are even more slippery on wet decks. There are numerous brands of effective nonskid soles available at supply stores, and they are a must on a boat. (Topsiders are considered ideal by most sailors.)

Gloves can be useful in cold weather, but they detract from the "feel" so often necessary for the hands on tiller and sheet, and they must therefore be used with caution. Only highly insulated gloves provide real warmth, since other types, perhaps better in appearance, cannot stand the rigors afloat.

Equipment

The U.S. Coast Guard publishes the following list of equipment legally requisite on boats of the size category treated in this book.

One life preserver for each person aboard
Fog horn
Bell
Anchor and anchor line
Lights for night sailing
Fire extinguisher (if engine carried)
Registration (in states which require same)

Fines for noncompliance are stiff.

Required by common sense if not by the Coast Guard are:

Copy of the U.S. Coast Guard Rules of the Road
Paddle, or oars
Boat hook
At least 2, but preferably 4 bumpers (fenders)
At least 4 dock lines

Copy of pilot rules
Copy of tide tables
Chart of waters to be crossed in any projected outing

Other equipment needed to operate the boat will be included in the boat purchase. It is wise to have an expert check the entire equipment list prior to signing any purchase contract.

Check sails periodically for rips, tears, and worn spots. Wash the sails each fall with fresh water and small amounts of mild detergent. Store them for the winter only when thoroughly dry.

Choice of Sails

In a catboat, there is no choice of sails to be made; only one sail is available. A sloop may be sailed either cat-rigged (with mainsail only) or with small front sail as well. In this book, most instructions are for a cat-rigged sloop. If one understands a cat-rigged sloop, there is but a minimal transition to a more complicated rig, or to using front sails.

Although a sloop is most efficient when using both sails, a normally designed sloop will sail well with the mainsail only; i.e., it will sail with full control and without disturbing idiosyncrasies.

One can anticipate in a cat-rigged sloop a more definite tendency to steer toward the wind, seldom a problem and often very useful. At worst, this characteristic in a cat-rigged sloop is but little greater than that in a plain catboat, and catboats have survived with great vitality through a good many decades of development.

Using only the mainsail for the first 8-10 hours of sailing practice will provide the beginner with increased simplicity of handling and greater visibility ahead. When the basic principles of sailing are fairly well taken for granted, the addition

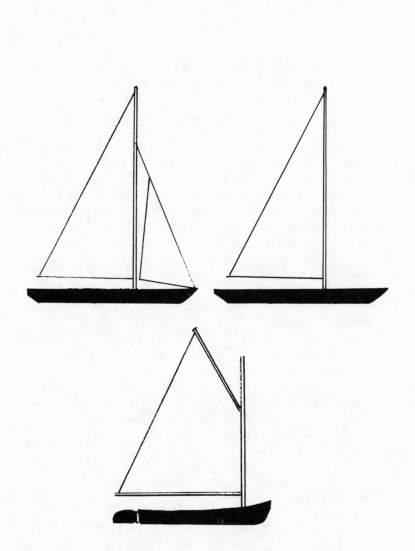

Figure 10-1. Types of sailboats.
Top left: Sloop. *Top right:* Cat-rigged sloop. *Bottom:* Catboat.

of one or more sails will become enjoyable, and they will drive the boat faster. This topic is treated in Chapter 13.

Locating Sails, Hardware, and Ropes

If the sail is wrapped (furled) on the boom, there is no location problem. One need merely remove sail cover and straps (sail stops) to be ready for raising sail. However, many small boat owners prefer to remove the sail entirely from the mast and boom and keep it in a bag. On small boats this solution requires little more time than furling does, and the sail is under cover and removed from rain and smog fallout.

Most sloops will have more than one small sail (jib)—working jib, which is the everyday sail, a Genoa jib, which is a much larger sail for fast sailing or racing, and possibly a spinnaker, for fast sailing when the wind is from behind the boat.

If all these sails are in bags, the sailor must select from the various bags the one he wants. Fortunately, each bag is stenciled. For instance, the large sail, or mainsail, will be stenciled "mainsail" (pronounced "mains'l").

Unfortunately, there is no stenciled guide on hardware or rope, although some sailors do label cleats and blocks with the function for which they are used. Four ropes (hereafter called "lines" in sailor fashion) are needed for cat-rigged sailing: the one for raising the sail (halyard, from old-timer's "haul yard"), the one for adjusting the sail angle (sheet, or mainsheet, when specific to the mainsail), the one for stretching the sail outwards on the boom (outhaul), and the one for pulling the gooseneck down (downhaul).

The mainsheet is easy: it is the only major line leading from boom to boat. On a sloop the halyard may be more difficult to pinpoint, since there will be several halyards, for raising jibs and/or spinnaker. There is no standardization for location of halyards, although perhaps the majority of rigs have the main halyards on the right side and the jib halyards on the left. In some boats the halyards terminate in a cleat on the mast; in other boats they terminate in cleats located back of the mast after passing through a block on deck. Almost all halyards on boats longer than twenty feet are linked with winches for increasing pulling power. To raise the mainsail requires location of the pertinent halyard and its winch and cleat.

To select the correct halyard from several, the best technique is to analyze continuity. If the sailor pulls on one halyard end and the wrong "other end" moves in result, he has hold of the wrong line. Sometimes the sail end (shackle end) of a halyard will have been "put to bed" close to the gooseneck and will therefore be easy to find. Often, however, it is simpler to secure the shackle end at some distance from the boom, perhaps in proximity to another halyard or similar-appearing line. To locate the shackle end of the main halyard, simply look to the back side of the top of the mast; the main halyard will be seen to emerge. From there it is simple to follow the line to its shackle by eye. Having thus found one end, the sailor can discover the other end by visual continuity or by untying all halyards (lines terminating on or near the mast) from their cleats and then pulling on the shackle end. Movement will be seen in the other end of the desired line. All other halyards should then be resecured to their cleats. A winch belonging to a given halyard will be located in line between the last block and the terminal cleat.

In some cases it can be difficult to determine which end of a given halyard is the pulling end, which the sail end; sometimes sailors tie them to the same fixture. To solve this, look aloft to the top of the mast, as noted above; then trace that stretch of line to its end. Or, look for the fiber rope end, which will be the pulling end, or the wire rope end, which will be the sail end. The wire is used to minimize stretching when the sail is pulling (fiber rope stretches far more than does wire rope). Of course, a further clue is in the ends themselves: the sail end will be fastened to a shackle of some type, whereas the pulling end has no fitting.

Bending on the Sail

"Bending" seems a strange word to use for the wondrously limber and remarkably strong materials used in sailmaking today. However, the word remains from the day when large heavy canvas sails were placed and replaced on spars in icy weather.

When dealing with a sail in a bag, the sailor first dumps that sail unceremoniously out of the bag onto the most handy surface, usually in the cockpit or on one side of the deck or cabin structure near the gooseneck area.

Next he locates the three corners of the sail in order to position it properly. One corner goes to the masthead, another to the end of the boom, and the third stays at the juncture of mast and boom. Usually the corner most easily identified is the one for the juncture of the two spars, since it is here that the sailmaker usually applies his label. This corner of the sail is always closest to being a right angle. Since the label is sewn or printed on horizontally, not only is the juncture corner located, but the entire sail becomes oriented. However, if the sailor sees one of the other corners first, the masthead one is identifiable from a stiffener (headboard) sewn into the cloth, while the third corner has no specific identification.

Before rigging the sail onto the spars, a good sailor overhauls the mast and boom edges hand over hand to be sure no turns or twists are likely to cause trouble. Twists appear most often on the mast edge, since this is the longest one, and more often in the upper part of this edge, where the sail is narrowest.

The best location from which to begin rigging the sail onto the spars is on one side of the mast near the gooseneck, since the sail will be introduced onto both spars from this location.

Spars are fitted with one of several devices which allow the entire edge of a sail to remain securely fastened and yet permit the sail to be raised or lowered quickly and surely. One device is a track on the spar on which slides sewn to the sail move easily. Another contrivance is a tunnel in the spar with a slot wide enough (3/16" or so) to permit passage of the sail cloth. The rope to which the sail is sewn rides in the tunnel, while the sail itself comes out through the slot. A third arrangement crosses the slide with the tunnel: the sail has cylindrical solid plastic slugs which slide inside the tunnel.

A quick glance determines whether the spars have tracks or tunnels, while another glance at the sail edges reveals the presence of slides, rope only or slugs.

Rigging the sail to the spars is simple. It is a good idea to arrange things so that the sail is between your body and the mast. This will keep the wind from grabbing a corner of the sail and making off with it or blowing it partially over the side and into the water. A wet sail is inconvenient and sloppy, though not a disaster. Very small centerboard boats may be too tippy to permit you to feed the sail onto the track or into the slot while standing next to the mast. In these boats, pile the sail in the forward part of the cockpit and feed it from there.

Most sailors favor putting the bottom of the sail on first, simply because in so doing the sail is spread over a wider area and thus most of the sail's bulk is removed from the next working area.

If the boom has a track, the sail slides on the boom edge are placed on the track one at a time, starting, of course, with the one which will be at the back end of the boom. If the rig is a tunnel, introduce the far end of the sail first and pull the

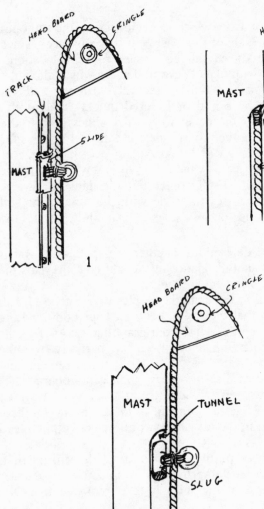

Figure 10-2. Arrangements for bending on the sail.
1. Track and slide. 2. Tunnel and bolt rope. 3. Tunnel and slug. (Note: Arrangements 1 and 2 can be for boom also.)

balance of that edge along after it. Sail edges in tunnels can bind in the pulling out process. You can eliminate binds by leading the edge of the sail into the tunnel from a position a few inches ahead of and somewhat below the entrance to the tunnel.

When starting the mast edge, the same technique will apply as indicated for the boom. In cruising boats you will far more likely encounter slides or slugs than bolt rope on the mast edge. This is because when using bolt ropes in tunnels, the sail must be either fully raised or fully on deck, an insurmountable problem when keeping a mainsail furled on the spars. With slides or slugs the mast edge can be mounted at any time because you can do this without spreading any sail to the wind. The length of sail edge between one slide or slug and the next is such that the sail cloth may be draped accordionlike, while only the small combined length of the slides or slugs controls the distance the sail must be pulled up to get it all onto the mast. A bolt rope/tunnel mast edge means that you should wait till last to start putting that edge on the mast. There will still be items on your checkoff list which can be handled more easily without having the sail raised and flapping or threatening to get "into gear" before you want it to.

At this point the sail is on the spars, or ready to be, but the corners are not yet fastened. The juncture corner is the first to be secured. There are jaws on the gooseneck designed to accept the brass-bound hole in the sail corner, termed a "cringle." Through holes in the jaws a pin is inserted to secure the fastening. Next the cringle at the end of the boom is secured. As previously noted, the rig used for stretching that edge of the sail is called an outhaul (because it *hauls* the sail *out* on the boom). A piece of line will be run through a hole or a block in the end of the boom. At one end this line will attach to the sail; at the other to a cleat. Different boats have different means of fastening the sail corner, but each is logical and easy to understand. The idea is to pull the sail hand-taut, not to stretch it with full strength.

In cleating the outhaul hand-taut, the sailor must engage a piece of line onto a cleat. There are two ways to do this, of which one is correct for lines such as halyards and control lines (sheets), which are likely to require quick emergency adjustment, the other correct for lines such as dock lines and outhauls which present no need for fast release in an emergency. In both, the line is first brought along the side of the cleat, turned under one arm of the T and then "figure-eighted" back and over, under back and over as shown in Figure 6-3. The two methods differ only in the means of finishing the tie to the cleat.

Both techniques of cleating are shown in Figure 6-3. The left center drawing in Figure 6-3 shows the line finally frictioned under the other turns on the cleat, very quick to undo but quite secure; the right center drawing in Figure 6-3 shows an additional hitch, in which the line is crossed over itself as the last turn is worked over the cleat. This hitch exerts more friction as the tension on it increases, thereby offering maximum security. However, when wet and cold, the final hitch takes a second or more to undo, and that may be just enough to allow trouble to start. The risk is least with artificial fiber lines; most with manila, linen, or cotton, since these shrink and grow shorter when wet. The hitch can be done correctly or incorrectly. The correct way is to turn the line so that the end comes out parallel to the other turns on the cleat which emanate from the same side of the T. Avoid crossing the hitch, as this eliminates most of the friction security.

The next item on the agenda is to insert the battens. Most mainsails have a curved back edge to attain more driving area. This curved part usually needs a little help to keep it from collapsing, which would rob power. The help is furnished by thin wooden or plastic strips which are inserted into pockets sewn into the sail. These strips are called battens. (See Figure 6-1.)

Some of the smaller sails have the battens sewn in permanently. However, the battens in most sails are removed to avoid breakage during bagging. A quick look at the back edge of your sail will identify your situation. If there are no pockets, your sail was not designed for battens. If there are pockets and the battens are sewn in, you still have nothing to do in this department. If the sail has empty pockets, you must find the battens and insert them.

Smaller boats have from two to four battens. Boats in the larger day-sailing and cruising categories almost universally have four. Few sails have battens all of the same length. Because of the lenticular shape of the curved back edge (roach), the shorter battens go top and bottom, longer ones between.

Battens may be wooden or plastic. Wooden ones are slightly tapered. Insert them tapered end first.

Battens are held within the pockets, after insertion, either with short bits of line or by a clever Y-shaped pocket arrangement, in which the batten enters via the top leg and while sailing is secured within the lower leg, which is sewn closed.

The sail is now "bent" on, and requires only raising to engage the power of the wind.

Facing the Boat to the Wind

When sailing from a beach or launching ramp, it is necessary to face the front of the boat into the wind before attempting to rig or sail it. This may require facing the boat away from, along, or toward the beach.

At anchor or at a mooring there is, of course, no problem. If there is wind enough to sail, the wind will align the boat automatically, just as it aligns a weather vane. The boat is tethered by a line at its bow; hence the wind can act only to move the stern away, downwind. Since all sails are "hinged" to the mast by track and slides, by rope or slugs in tunnel, or (in the case of jibs) by hooks onto the stay, the boat must point to the wind in order to insure that the fixed edge of the sail also points to the wind. Remember that the sail exerts no power when this leading edge faces the wind and forces it to pass over *both* surfaces equally. If the boat faced across the wind, the sail could quite easily engage the full power of the wind. If the boat pointed downwind, again the sail could fill, often with nearly unmanageable consequences.

If the boat is berthed at a fixed location, such as a dock, float, or slip, it is quite routine to come for a sail and find the boat facing downwind or across the wind. Alignment is accomplished as in the following examples.

If at a float or dock and the wind blows from the stern, release all dock lines except the one from the bow. Almost immediately the wind will start blowing the boat downwind. As its stern comes around, start walking, while holding onto the bow line, toward the area from which the stern came. By the time that short walk is complete, the boat will have reversed its heading and the job is done. If bumpers (antichafe gear hung from sailboat at points where chafing is expected) have been in use, transfer them to the side now adjoining the dock. If you plan to go sailing soon, it is not necessary to secure more than the bow line, since the wind will keep the boat "head to wind."

If at a float or dock and the wind blows across the boat *from* the dock, it is again necessary only to release all lines except the bow line. The wind will then stream the boat away from the dock and you must board it from the bow. If the boat is small enough to prove unstable when a person's weight is located at the bow, pull the boat more parallel to the dock before boarding.

If at float or dock and the wind blows across the boat *toward* the dock, new difficulties arise for the inexperienced

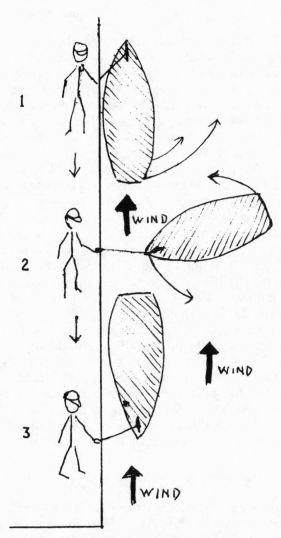

Figure 10-3. Facing the boat to the wind.
If boat is facing downwind, proceed as follows: 1. Loose all lines except the one at the front of the boat. 2. Let the wind blow the back of the boat out from the dock and toward where the front was. 3. As this is happening, walk upwind. Very quickly the boat will lie alongside, facing the wind.

sailor. If the sail were inadvisedly raised in this situation, the force of the wind would blow directly against its total area, since the boom could not be free to weathercock or blow downwind because of the intervening pilings or posts, side of the dock, or other protuberances. And, even with a dock free from such things, the wind force will press the boat quite solidly against the side of the dock or float. Trying to sail away from a dock while being blown against it is a near impossibility. However, the following paragraphs on berthing in a slip will furnish some ideas for handling this situation also.

Because of the nature of a slip, designed as it is to "park" a boat in the smallest possible space, it is almost impossible to move the boat to head into the wind and still stay within the enclosure. This is, of course, complicated by the fact that it is normal to finish an outing by steering the boat into the slip bow-first. Sometimes a powerboat will back in, but sailboats reverse poorly under power and so are seldom backed into close quarters.

If the wind is from the side, the sail cannot go free on either side because of the pilings which form the slip. With the wind blowing toward the slip, or toward the boat's stern, the only recourses are engines, paddles, or the simple process of "walking" the boat along the pilings until her heading can be changed. This is feasible only in light winds. There is no rule which states that one must raise sail inside the slip. Paddle out a good distance, if you want the exercise.

The Pros and Cons of Using Power

This book is an introduction to sailing, not power boating. The sailor who can sail his boat without power under all circumstances is the sailor who will most enjoy the sport and who will feel secure in the knowledge that his skill alone is adequate to ensure the safety of boat and passengers.

Of course, the most tempting times to turn on the engine

are when you leave the dock or mooring and when you return to it. Many sailors use power every time they go out and come back. However, it is at these very times when power failure would most tax the sailor's skills. It is wise, therefore, that from the very beginning you learn how to handle your boat all the way without power.

Obviously, this no-power idea can be carried too far. If there's a calm or if the current is moving in a direction seriously impeding the course to your destination, use power.

The point is that since you are learning to harness wind, it makes sense to use wind whenever possible. Naturally, if you have an engine, care for it well so it can be counted on in emergencies.

Coiling Lines

Before engaging the power of the sail by raising it, all lines should be coiled neatly and compactly so that they are ready to run free when needed. When you board a new or strange boat, check to make sure that lines, halyards in particular, have figure-eight knots in their ends. This is to insure against their being pulled through the blocks and out of reach—aloft if halyards are external to the mast, and inaccessibly up and inside the mast for internal halyards. Tying the figure-eight knot is no trouble (see Chapter 6), and it can save a lot of trouble and lost sailing time.

As for coiling of lines, there is nothing more disconcerting than trying to use a line which has been improperly coiled. Murphy's Law ("If something can go wrong, it will!") causes a turn or even a knot to appear in the thing, and it will not go through the block or leader (fairlead). Or, it lies in a messy heap underfoot and snags your ankle.

In a correctly piled coil, the working part leads from the top of the coil so that when the line is pulled it will come freely and exhibit no tendency to engage any lower loops.

(See Knots and Ties in Chapter 6 for proper coiling techniques.)

Lowering the Centerboard

The board should be lowered before you get in the boat at dockside or at the mooring, or as soon after you board the boat as possible. The centerboard in the down position prevents the boat from rocking excessively and dampens out the motion caused by you or others as you climb around the boat making ready to go for a sail. However, with the board down at a mooring, a slant of wind from the side can start the boat sailing around the mooring. Raising the board for a moment will allow the boat quickly to weathercock again until you are ready to start sailing.

If you are moored or berthed in shallow water and the board touches bottom when part way down, it may be possible to sail out with care by using the partially lowered centerboard in the farthest down position you can put it. If you have doubts, lower the sail and paddle the boat or motor it in the direction of deeper water, and raise the sail there.

In a keel boat, when you sense it is touching bottom, you may have to wait for a rise in the tide. Other approaches involve tilting or heeling the boat by hanging out on the sidestays and paddling, towing, or even sailing the boat towards deeper water. When sailing is attempted, and when traffic conditions allow, sailing across the wind maximizes sail horsepower or drive, and thereby increases assistance from the sail itself to achieve tilt or heel and reduce the dragging of the keel on the bottom.

chapter 11

Heading for the Open Water

If the reader has absorbed the information on preparation for sailing contained in the preceding chapters and will master the information on "doing" which follows, he will have no trouble even on his first sail.

To sail a boat from one place to another with no "on the job" teaching may be learned by simple trial and error, or by studious application to intellectual preparation. The latter is safer and less costly.

Sailing is essentially the skill of coordinating many uncomplicated thoughts and actions. Reading about sailing makes it look more complicated than it is, but reading about it helps uncomplicate the doing of it. Planning ahead for all maneuvers is the best "uncomplicator."

Making Allowances for Traffic and Current

Even someone fortunate enough to keep his boat in an area free of traffic, anchorage density, and tidal currents and yet sheltered from high waves, as anchorages mostly are, may some day soon find himself visiting an anchorage with a combination of such problems. Consider a situation quite prevalent these days:

Your mooring is in the midst of a large fleet of anchored boats, of all sizes and shapes. Some of these boats are preparing to leave their moorings. Dinghies are traveling from dock to mooring. A yacht club launch is running from club to yacht and from yacht to yacht, delivering members to their boats. However, you are fortunate because the tide is slack, allowing the boats to lie head to wind and not complicating passage to open water.

An exit plan is easier to formulate before raising sail than after. What is the wind direction? Does it favor the easy way out by reaching or running? If not, how close to the wind can the first tack be planned? At what point must the next tack be executed? Is the wind gusty? If so, its direction will change often and precipitately, with attendant need for plan revision. (Plan revision is easier if one expects the need to revise.) Where will the boats now preparing to leave their moorings be when you are out there? Will the dinghies all be visible, or will one or more suddenly appear from behind a moored boat?

Another item to consider is the length of mooring lines through the harbor. A mooring line consists of an anchor line from bottom to deck, but sometimes these are very long, particularly if an inexperienced owner has set the mooring anchor himself. Mostly these lines are marked at the water surface by a float, from which leads the line which is made fast on the boat's deck. Sometimes this combination is further complicated by the use of a "pickup" float, usually with a long whiplike protrusion making it simpler to pick up a mooring from a high deck when returning from a sail. In sum, moorings can be very long, and it is obviously unwise to go between a moored yacht and any of its floating mooring

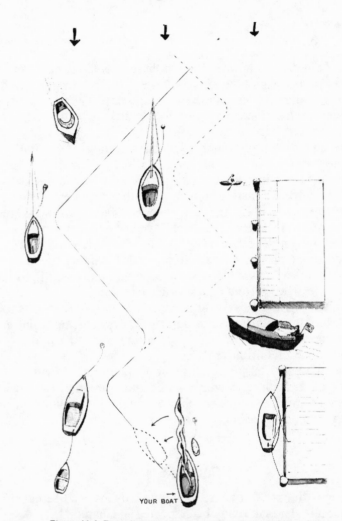

YOUR BOAT

Figure 11-1. Threading through an anchorage outward bound.
The drawing illustrates the most difficult way of leaving a dock or mooring, i.e., beating. As shown, your boat is the one in the middle at the bottom of the drawing. You have just let go of the mooring line, leaving the dinghy tied to the mooring. Since the dinghy is on your right, you begin with a tack toward the left. You could have selected the opposite tack, but didn't because the dock at the right is closer than the moored boat on the left. The solid line represents the course you choose, the dotted line the course you might have chosen. The course you choose is the better one, based on the location of obstacles such as the power boat leaving a dock, the dinghy being rowed to a moored boat, etc.

aids. Sometimes the lines linking these aids are sunken out of sight. Sometimes the whole complex is further lengthened by having a dinghy tied astern of the moored yacht on a long painter. Each mooring situation must be observed and analyzed with care.

Planning to leave when tidal current flows fast requires consideration of a new technique: allowing for drift. When the tide is flowing, the entire expanse of water is moving— faster in deeper water, slower near shore and over shoals. Hence, when sailing through moving water, a boat's true course is the result of a boat speed vector and a current speed vector. In simpler terms, there is sidewise drift when crossing the current (same as a river), forward drift (higher speed over the bottom) when sailing with the current, and possibly backward drift when sailing against the current.

In the light winds recommended, it may be unwise for beginners to venture out through dense traffic without power, since the boat may not be able to attain a speed equal to or greater than that of the current.

No matter which direction the flow, one must allow for the effect of drift on the boat's speed and direction, to avoid collisions with stationary objects, such as anchored and moored boats, docks, and shoals.

Raising Sail

Sailing with mainsail alone, only one halyard need be considered, and this has already been located in Chapter 10.

After casting the sheet loose in order to allow the sail to travel freely with wind shifts, "start the engine" by simply hoisting the sail to the top of the mast, making the halyard fast on its cleat, and tying the downhaul down hand-taut. In larger boats (over twenty feet), a winch may be helpful in raising the sail fully. Always put the halyard around the winch clockwise. Use three or more turns. Then coil the halyard end and hang it from its cleat, ready for immediate use. (See Figure 6-5.)

Cast a quick glance toward the tiller to be doubly sure that it is not in any way impeded from moving; the rudder must be free to swing when the boat swings with wind shifts. Also look at the telltales. Are they free to signal wind shifts? Take a look at the centerboard. Is it at the desired height? Check the pendant holding the boom end, or the boom crutch. Is this device free and clear? Most importantly, is the sheet untied and able to run free?

Freeing Lines

Even with the boat aligned to face the wind, minor changes in wind direction must be expected because they are commonplace. The sailboat requires time to follow the wind shifts, which are often quite sudden (as anyone who has observed the nervousness of a weather vane knows). During the short interval of time while the boat attempts to realign its heading, the wind approaches the boat (and sails) at an angle. Because the sail will exert power when the wind strikes it at an angle, steps must be taken to insure against untimely sail power. Having freed the sheet now prevents such inadvertent takeoffs, because the sail is unfettered and will be blown away from the wind and remain in neutral.

Casting Off

Towing a dinghy while learning to sail is an unnecessary distraction. Leave it at the mooring.

The first consideration in leaving the dinghy is which side of the sailboat to put it on. If placed on the side toward which the first course is planned, it will be a distinct liability.

When the mooring line was brought aboard after the last

sail, it might have been led through the bow chock, which is now on the side toward the first course. Hence, if the dinghy is correctly brought to the opposite side, its painter must be led *around* the headstay before being secured to the mooring line. If you lead the painter directly to the mooring line on deck, you may find to your dismay on attempting to cast off that you have in effect "sewn" the boat into the mooring system by the headstay, with the dinghy fighting to climb up on deck from one side, and the mooring line straining downward into the water on the other side of your bow. This is embarrassing but not dangerous. Why not lead the painter properly the first time?

The mooring line generally ends in an eye (spliced or tied loop). It is to this loop that the dinghy painter will be tied. If the painter is long, it should be tied near its midpoint by the use of two half hitches with the doubled-over line. If the painter is short, secure it with a bowline or a clove hitch with an added hitch around the standing part of the lead to the dinghy for insurance. (See Figure 6-2 for illustrations of the pertinent knots.) Having secured the dinghy while the sailboat is still firmly tethered (letting the mooring line go *before* tying the dinghy to it is asking for unnecessary pressures), cast off.

At this point the sail is head to wind, with tiller and sheet free, and hence "in neutral." Without turning the boat to a point at which the sail angle can harness the wind, the boat would simply drift backward with no control. (Remember that without forward speed a rudder cannot steer.) For small boats there is a simple technique for acquiring sufficient forward speed: after taking the mooring loop from the cleat or bitt and clearing it from the chock, simply walk back toward the cockpit with the mooring line firmly held in your hand. In effect, this action tows the boat toward the mooring, but, even more importantly, the action moves the securing point from the bow to the middle of the boat. This allows the boat to pivot and turn away from the wind. Make sure, of course, that the tiller is angled to help this turn, not hinder it.

An alternative technique for getting the sailboat moving, particularly in small, light boats which do not allow for the sailor's weight near the bow, is to get into the dinghy, move the dinghy to the desired side of the bow, tie the painter as noted above, unfasten the mooring line from cleat or bitt, then push the sailboat ahead by moving it past the dinghy until the cockpit comes alongside. The same amount of movement and pivoting will result as noted above. However, *don't* ever fail to make it aboard your sailboat from the dinghy.

If the casting off is from a dock, the procedure is extremely simple: merely let go the line securing the boat to the dock, push off, and sail.

As stated earlier, from a slip, in almost all cases auxiliary propulsion will be needed. A paddle can do well in a small boat. An engine in a larger boat can be used to get to a good spot for raising sail. (The sail is never raised while the boat is inside the slip.)

Now you are ready to feel the power in that wind/sail engine you are learning to control.

Anxieties, Anyone?

People sailing for the first time often feel anxiety. It is far better to admit this to one's self than to move forward with bravado alone. Knowing that others feel the same anxiety—and they do—will help allay the queasiness the reader may experience the first few times out.

Threading Through the Anchorage

If the wind is from the side of the planned course, there is no complication at all. Just steer the boat onto the desired course and trim the sheet to an efficient setting.

If the wind is blowing *toward* one's objective, or planned sailing area, the only possible complication is an inadvertent jibe caused by a wind shift. One must be on the watch for wind shifts. Actually, in light to moderate airs it is quite permissible to leave the mooring and thread through the fleet with the sheet trimmed well in. By so doing, the sailor contains the boat's "width" by eliminating the extra spread of a boom trimmed fully out. With the boom in, a jibe is mild. However, this shortcut should not be attempted in light centerboard boats when the breeze is fresh. Also, in a head (foul) tide, this inefficient trim may sacrifice too much speed.

If the wind is coming *from* the objective, thus requiring a beat through the fleet, prior planning will have charted the outline of courses. Drifting, unanticipated traffic, and wind shifts will require on-the-spot changes in plan. In making judgments for corrective courses, perhaps the most important "don't" to keep in mind is "Don't allow the boat to luff *at any time,* even when steering directly at an obstruction." Luffing kills speed, and speed is necessary for steering. Hence, luffing means quick loss of control, and loss of control results in aimless drifting—just the wrong thing for crowded quarters. Instead, select the better of two options: come about and get the boat moving quickly on the other tack, or steer away from the wind (bear off) enough to clear the obstruction. Bearing off does not lose speed, but in small boats it is well to ease the sheet out a little while bearing off.

In crowded quarters it is not essential to sail the boat at the optimum angle of forty-five degrees to the wind, since the primary purpose is not efficiency in getting to an objective but instead is keeping boat speed while plotting a circuitous course. Of course, the deviation from forty-five degrees must be in moderation, or sailing the circuitous course will become the end and not the means; the day will be spent in the anchorage, tacking back and forth on a reciprocal course.

It is good practice to keep the sheet in the hand, not cleated, whenever in close quarters, even in light winds. This is mandatory in light, centerboard boats.

Once moving on a beat, the boat will heel. Heeling may, of course, be stopped by either heading slightly closer to the wind or by easing out the sheet. When heeling in crowded quarters, remember that, although the hull may be at a safe distance from another boat, the top of your mast may be very close to the other boat's rigging. Your weight on the windward (top) side will be helpful in controlling heel angle.

One final factor to watch out for in sailing through crowded quarters: all the boats anchored or moored will be swinging in a slow-paced arc which varies with current eddies and wind shifts. To avoid collisions in negotiating an anchorage, keep alert.

chapter 12

Berthing Like a Pro

Even the sailor who has learned well the basics contained in the preceding chapters must plan each trip from takeoff to landing to be sure of an expeditious, trouble-free return home. He must master the steps involved in landing the boat as routine procedure rather than a practice exercise. However, now that he has become familiar with the way his boat responds to his direction and has thoroughly practiced the basic sailing maneuvers, landing will be easy.

To plan his return well, the sailor must consider the following factors: wind direction, the location of all moving and moored boats, the landin: pattern, securing the boat, and tidying up.

Wind Direction

If the wind has maintained its general direction all during the sail now coming to a close, the sailor will need little time for applying that direction to plans for returning. However, if a shift has come about, returning through the traffic will require new course(s) and changed sail trim(s). The sailor should establish the entire course diagram in his mind before undertaking the return. With the mental course diagram must go an idea of the right sail trim for each course and change of direction.

If helpful to planning at leisure, the sailor can always make his boat "lie to" on "automatic pilot" (see Chapter 9) as long as needed for basic landing preparations: put out bumpers (fenders) and get dock lines ready for use as needed, get the boat hook free and ready for use (it is a most effective arm extension), and double-check that the main halyard is properly coiled without tangles and is free and ready to run out.

Traffic

Boats will be approaching and leaving the anchorage and docks. Moored boats will have changed their position if the wind has changed in direction, or if the tide has changed and is acting on these boats. The pattern of moored boats will look quite different entering a harbor from the way it looked in leaving.

However, all anchorages are laid out with plenty of space between moored and anchored boats of all sizes. The sailor must simply find the widest spaces best located for the course planned.

Keep an eye peeled at all times for moving vessels of all sizes, including dinghies. Be sure to leave room for the heeling angle of your own boat. Remember that the top of your mast may be angled a number of feet to the side of the course sailed, while the masts of moored boats are vertical.

Landing Pattern

The landing pattern includes not only the movement through traffic but the selection of location for final approach and final landing. The treatment of landing techniques here amplifies the instructions under Practice Landings in Chapter 9 because practice landings are done in open water while final landings are executed in crowded quarters.

Since the pattern will need a base leg and a final approach leg, there must be space for these legs plus at least one turn. The legs may be long or short as space limitations permit, but they must be precisely worked out. Many people feel anxious about the final landing, perhaps because that requires contact, but they should actually pay more attention to the *landing pattern,* because it controls the landing's success.

During the landing pattern, which includes the passage through traffic toward the points selected for the base leg and final approach, the sailor may need to use his knowledge of tacking, jibing, smooth turns, sail trim, tiller handling, headreaching, getting out of irons, turn radius, and heel control.

If the wind comes from the dock or mooring area, there is no alternative to beating through the fleet, a course which will call upon all the knowledge one has. Reaching and running produce only minor problems. In reaching, the skipper may counteract excessive speed by spilling the wind from the sail—letting out the sheet. With the sail and boom way out, the boat uses more lateral space but heeling is minimal; so the mast is nearly vertical. When running through a fleet in light to moderate winds, the sailor may pull the boom in over the boat with resultant major space-saving. Decreasing the driving power of the sail in this way results in reduced speed, which is often a desirable element of control.

One very important item in review: if the landing pattern

requires beating through traffic, *don't cheat by trying to stretch a tack upwind of an obstacle.* Either come about or steer downwind around the obstacle.

The base leg and final approach leg simply constitute a controlled pattern for getting in irons at dockside or at the mooring.

If the boat's forward motion stops too soon, the skipper must employ corrective action to regain boat speed and to restart the landing pattern. If the final approach speed is "too hot," a light boat can often be stopped by sheer muscle power at dockside, simply by holding onto any available protuberance, such as a cleat. At a mooring, however, even a light boat will continue to headreach after a really fast landing, carrying the mooring float or dinghy along with it. The unpleasant result of this is usually that the boat fetches up at the end of the mooring's anchor line and then begins to sail in a circle around the anchor; a full circle entails a jibe, further sailing, tacking, further sailing, etc., until momentum is somehow stopped, usually by lowering the sail (which can be difficult if the sailor is at the same time hanging onto the mooring line or dinghy). In brisk breezes, "hot" landings definitely call for another pass at the landing, because the boat's high speed will cause heavy contact and possible damage.

The preceding considerations explain why light air sailing is best for the inexperienced. Only experience—trial and error—can develop judgment, and only judgment can produce consistently good landings in all weather conditions. The least troublesome mistake is a landing that is only slightly too fast, since it can be stopped without real problems, especially if the sailor has learned to use the mainsail and rudder as brakes.

The best assurance of a good landing is proper planning of the base leg/final approach pattern. The base leg, being at ninety degrees to final approach (and to the wind), will be sailed on a beam reach. Boat speed on this leg can be changed at will by sheet handling: to slow down, the skipper eases the sheet so that the sail luffs; to speed up, he trims the sail to optimum efficiency. The sailor must start the turn onto the final approach with sufficient anticipation to allow for the turning radius required by the kind of turn planned—if a hard turn, a very short radius; if an easy turn, a long radius. If the sailor waits until the wind axis has been reached, after the turn the boat will tend to go back on the other tack, sailing an S-curve to the landing spot. As noted in Chapter 9, Point X is not *on* the wind axis or final approach line but is a short distance out on the base leg.

The brake landing and the controlled-motion landing are excellent techniques as additional strings to the bow, but the sailor should learn the classic "in irons" landing first; it is harder in some ways, but it is feasible in some conditions which preclude the others.

If, despite all care and body English, your landing is not a "keeper," take the following corrective steps:

1) Use any desired technique to gain boat speed and rudder action.

2) Steer away from the dock or mooring far enough to permit a turn, a new base leg, and a final approach leg. The turn is usually a jibe, since you will wish to go downwind for a distance to locate the new base leg at good head-reaching distance from the dock or mooring.

Dock Landings

Additional considerations are involved in planning landings at docks. Whereas moorings have a 360-degree approach potential, docks offer only 180 degrees on only one side (floats may offer two or three sides if you are particularly fortunate). Further, that one side is fixed, regardless of wind shifts or other variables which affect approach patterns. There are several possibilities:

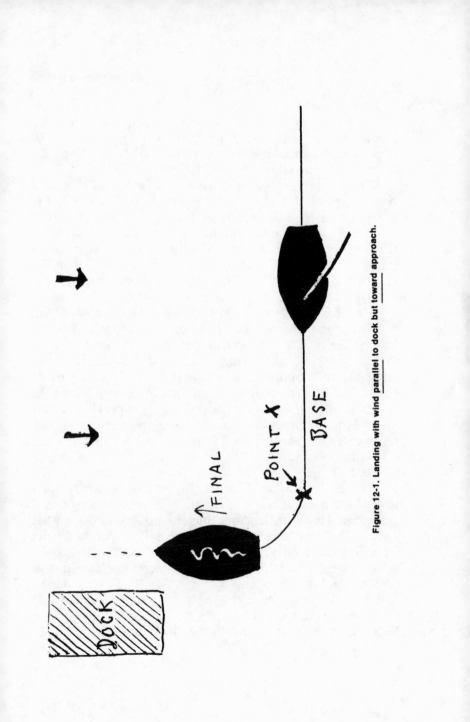

Figure 12-1. Landing with wind parallel to dock but toward approach.

Wind Parallel to Dock but Toward Approach. Lay out the base leg to bring the boat downwind of the near end of the landing surface and at a distance from it equal to the final approach (headreaching distance). Allowing for turning radius, make the final turn and head for the landing.

Wind Parallel to Dock but from Approach. Sail along and past the intended landing surface so as to get downwind of it. Lay out base leg and final approach leg from there. If space is limited, use brake landing as follows: sail along and past the dock at a distance allowing only for a hard-turn radius (not enough for a base leg); when downwind of the landing area, make a hard turn of 180 degrees. This will stop the boat quickly and in a very small space.

Wind Blowing Across Dock Toward Landing Side. Sail parallel to the landing surface, which will in effect place the boat on the base leg; then make the final approach turn so as to headreach for the landing area. In this situation, try to make the final approach at an angle to the landing surface (controlled-motion landing). A straight-in approach runs the risk of damage if overshot, whereas an angle provides a start into a turn and hence enables easier and quicker fending off. Of course, the sheet must be free to run so that the sail cannot be powered.

Wind Blowing Toward Dock from Approach. As the reader has learned in Chapter 10, when the wind blows toward the dock, it is not advisable to attempt leaving under sail alone. However, landings must be made no matter what wind shifts have occurred during the sailing period (if the wind has come on very strong, another location should be selected for landing). The following is accepted technique in normal wind strengths and is not difficult: (1) Get four to five boat lengths upwind of the dock landing surface. (2) Head the boat directly into the wind. (3) Drop the sail. The boat will then drift slowly to the dock and can be easily secured.

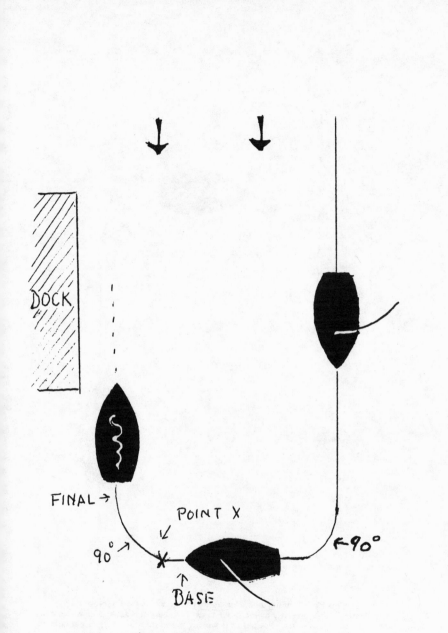

DOCK

FINAL →

POINT X

90°

←90°

BASE

Figure 12-2. Landing with wind parallel to dock but from approach.

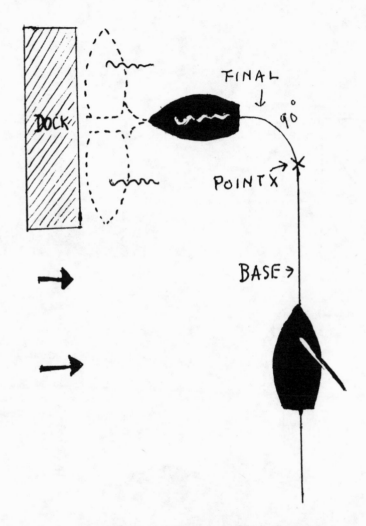

Figure 12-3. Landing with wind <u>across</u> dock and toward approach.
   It is better to turn one way or the other to avoid hitting the dock straight on. Also, in some small boats you cannot put your weight in the front in order to get onto the dock; so sidewise debarking is necessary.

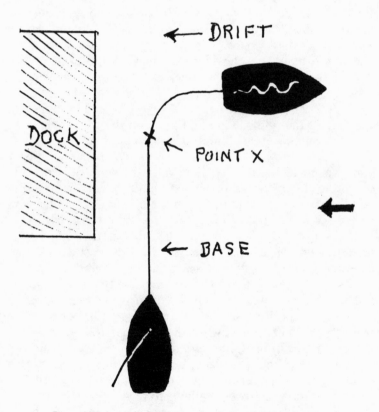

Figure 12-4. Landing with wind <u>across</u> dock and <u>from</u> approach.

No matter which landing pattern is required, the beginner should practice numerous landings each time out, at the dock or mooring.

Securing the Boat

After you have made the final practice landing for the day, you must still secure the boat safely.

If at a mooring, pick up the dinghy painter or mooring float with hands or boat hook. Then place the mooring line loop over the cleat or bitt near the bow. Make doubly certain that this loop is securely retained by the cleat or bitt. As added safeguard, tie the loop snugly onto the cleat or bitt with a short piece of light rope, to counteract any jerking caused by waves. Next, drop the sail to prevent all wind force from producing boat movement. Finally, bring the dinghy to the stern of the sailboat and tie its painter to a handy cleat.

If the sailboat is small and light, it might be quite inadvisable to attempt tying up by staying aboard. Instead, transfer your weight to the dinghy, hold onto the sailboat, work the dinghy to the sailboat's bow cleat or bitt, place the mooring line loop over that cleat or bitt, untie the dinghy painter, and work back to tie up the dinghy and reboard the sailboat.

If at a dock or float, jump off the sailboat, carrying a dock line already secured to the boat's bow cleat, just as the boat comes alongside the dock. Fasten the dock line to a cleat on the dock. Of course, the mainsheet must be free to run; so the sail will be in neutral during this maneuver. Next, reboard the boat and pull the sail down. If sailing with a crew, have one person lower the sail while the other carries the dock line ashore for securing. Experienced sailors favor lowering the sail during the final approach, but for the inexperienced this involves risk of undershooting with attendant loss of rudder control and no sail power available to regain that control.

As far as we have gone, landings and initial tying up are

handled the same whether at dock, float, or alongside another boat. However, securing the boat well enough to leave it untended for extended periods of time entails different dock line handling at a fixed dock from that required at a floating site (float or other vessel).

Floating landing sites rise and fall with the tide, and so do boats tied up to them. At fixed docks, the tide changes the water level relative to dock level.

Whereas a mooring requires only one line, any stationary landing surface requires several lines; any boat tied for a length of time at a dock by a single line risks damage from wind shifts.

Normally four lines are best:

1) Bow breast line, a line tied at the boat's bow and leading to a dockside cleat opposite or forward of the boat's bow cleat.

2) Stern breast line, a line tied at the boat's stern and leading to a dockside cleat opposite to or back of the stern cleat.

3) After bow spring, a line tied to a cleat in the forward third of the boat and leading to a dockside cleat near the stern of the boat.

4) Forward quarter spring, a line tied to a cleat in the stern third of the boat and leading to a dockside cleat near the boat's bow.

The spring lines keep the boat from moving frontwards or backwards, while the breast lines control lateral movement. The lines are secured in the order given.

At dockside and in slips, the sailor must also protect his boat against damage caused by the rise and fall of the tides. Correct length and angle of all dock lines allow the boat to move vertically without incurring damage. A very short line tied at high tide will certainly risk damaging the boat at low tide. An acute angle of dock line from boat cleat to dock cleat minimizes the need for extra line length to counteract lower tide levels.

The degree of care required in dock line length and angle is dictated by the maximum rise and fall of tides charted for a given waterway. (Tidal rise and fall varies daily. It becomes greatest at full moon and new moon periods, least at half-moon.)

Fiber line stretches by a percentage of its length. Hence, a 20-foot dock line will stretch more than a 10-foot line. Yet, there is a limit to the dock space which can be occupied by dock lines; so the sailor must provide line length by: (1) leading lines from the side of the boat farthest from the dock, thereby adding stretch and lowering lead angle without taking up any extra dock space; (2) leaving a length of slack in all lines appropriate to the rise and fall of the tide level existing at the time of the landing. Some dock lines have eye splices (loops) at one end. These loops are put over the dockside cleat or bitt and the other end used on board the boat. Wherever there is need to *tie* a dock line around a cleat or bitt, either on shore or on board, it is mandatory to use the hitch on the last crossover of the normal cleat technique (see Figure 6-3).

Passing boats cause wakes, and wind causes waves; a boat seldom rests quietly at the dock. Every time the boat moves with a wave, it jerks on the dock lines. Each tug puts sudden and severe loads not only on each line but on the method of securing it to the cleat. The line's elasticity will absorb some of this jerking, but each yank will nonetheless severely test the friction in the turns around the cleat; friction alone holds the boat, in the final analysis.

A further caution on the handling of dock lines: any line moving over any object will chafe. The more often it moves and the greater its tension, the more chafing will occur. Even a partially chafed line has lost a frighteningly high percentage of its designed strength. Hence, it is both economical and wise to use chocks in leading lines from the boat. Chocks hold the lines safe within their smooth-surface grip. If a line leads over any sharp or rough surface anywhere, wrap that segment with rags, a piece of sturdy canvas, a length of hose, or other chafing gear.

Tidying Up for the Next Time

The great majority of sailors pride themselves on keeping their boats neat and tidy by having a place for everything and everything in its place, whenever the boat is not in active use. A sailboat not so kept will be an eyesore in any fleet, not only unattractive but often unsafe. "Putting the boat to bed" is normally accomplished in the following order:

1) Secure the boom approximately parallel to the water. Some boats are fitted with lines, called "topping lifts," running from the top of the mast to the end of the boom. These lines are controllable, so that the boom may be raised or lowered to suit the convenience and comfort of the sailor. Other boats have pendants fastened to the backstay; a hook at the other end of each pendant fastens to the end of the boom. Still other boats have a scissorslike device, called a "boom crutch," "boom scissors," or "shear legs." The two long ends of this device are placed in small receptacles on the cockpit sole (floor), or on deck, depending on the boat, and the short ends are shaped to accept the boom. By whatever means, the boom will be easier to deal with if secured.

2) Pull in all slack in the mainsheet, secure it to its cleat, and coil the entire slack. Hang the coil on a convenient cleat or from the boom, whichever seems the more simple and sensible method.

3) Secure the sail. If it seems simpler to remove the sail entirely from the boom, reverse the steps used to put the sail on. Then put the sail in its bag. Some sailors simply start with

any corner and stuff the balance in after that corner. Others prefer to fold the sail into a tidy bundle and then insert it in the sail bag. The best way to learn the folding technique is to watch somebody else.

If there is a sail cover and it seems better to leave the sail on the boom, stand approximately one-third of the boom's length from the mast. Grab the sail at a point about two feet above the boom. Using this two-foot length of sail as a "bag," stuff the balance of the sail into it, fold the "bag" down over the works, and tie it all to the boom with pieces of strapping called "sail stops," lengths of shock cord, or plain rope. Four or five stops should be enough to form the sail into a neat, tight furl from gooseneck to boom end. The most care is generally needed at the gooseneck, where the greatest bulk of sail will be located.

4) Take the halyard from the top of the sail and hook it to any convenient device on the boat which does not move or stretch (turnbuckle, gooseneck, etc.). Tighten the halyard and cleat it down. In any mooring area near which people sleep it is good manners to tie all halyards away from the mast to prevent their slatting from the action of wind or waves. This is particularly important with aluminum masts, which make the slatting extremely noisy. Tie the halyards to the side stays with short lengths of light line or with shock cord.

5) Rig the sail cover. Start by laying it out along the length of the boom. Then fasten the collar around the mast. Finally, fasten each tie location, moving from mast to boom end, stretching the cover at the boom end for neatness.

6) Tie the tiller over the centerline. If this is not done, the rudder will be allowed to work back and forth on its hinge as the boat rocks, with resultant unnecessary wear of the rudder post bearing surface. The best bet for tying the tiller is a length of light line secured approximately opposite the end of the tiller to any device on deck or in the cockpit. Pass this

line around the tiller two or three times or use a clove hitch; then secure its other end to a cleat or other device on the opposite deck.

7) Make a careful visual check to see that all lines are secure and neatly coiled. Check dock line lengths and angles. Be sure that all valuables, either personal or belonging to the boat, are locked up out of sight or taken ashore.

chapter 13

How to Handle
Working Jibs

After a few hours of practice, sailing with mainsail alone will become routine, and the sailor will then enjoy learning to use the working jib.

The working jib, used for easy single-handed sailing and for brisk breezes, is a relatively small sail in area, but it has considerable effect on boat balance and speed. This is because all jibs do more than simply add area. By aerodynamic interaction between jib and mainsail, the jib increases the efficiency of the mainsail itself. Further, all jibs have almost twice the aerodynamic efficiency of the mainsail. The working jib is the best jib to use in getting acquainted with new sails.

Look for the working jib in a bag stenciled accordingly. A few sailmakers put working jibs and mainsails in the same bag and stencil to suit.

Take the bag to the foredeck (in front of the mast) in boats large enough to allow weight up there; in smaller boats set the jib from the cockpit. Dump the sail out of the bag and throw the bag into the cockpit.

Orienting the Jib

As with the mainsail, the three corners are identifiable. The lower front corner has the sailmaker's label; the lower back corner has nothing but a cringle. Most jibs have wire rope along the leading edge, or luff; it is most important that the luff of a jib be kept tight, and fiber rope stretches. Instead of a headboard at the top corner, jibs have a thimble around which the top of the luff wire is eye-spliced.

Fasten the lower front corner to the device located in the center of the bow, very close to the stem (farthest forward part of the boat). A shackle will be found either on that device or in the jib cringle. Fasten the jib halyard to the thimble at the top jib corner.

Locating the Sheets

Locate the working jib sheets. There are usually two because most jibs require one sheet leading to each side. These sheets will be either one single line with a shackle or hook in the middle for the jib's lower back corner, or two separate lines fastened to a common ring or shackle in the middle. It is important that both sheets be worked through the leads located for the working jib.

Raising the Jib

When all three corners of the jib are properly located and hooked up, haul the halyard to raise the jib. It is important for aerodynamic efficiency to apply considerable tension on the jib halyard so that no slack, or scalloping, may be seen in the luff. In most boats over sixteen feet a winch is provided to assist in obtaining good halyard tension. Secure the halyard to its pertinent cleat and coil the free end so that it will be immediately and easily usable.

It is, of course, most likely that the jib will be set and raised at the mooring or while on "automatic pilot" outside of the anchorage. To get the boat going, simply pull the jib sheet on the side opposite to the direction planned for the first sailing course. The jib will thus engage the wind and will blow the boat's bow in the desired direction. Both mainsail and jib may then be trimmed to suit the point of sailing to be used—beat, reach, or run.

Setting Mainsail and Jib

Start by setting the mainsail correctly; then set the jib so that it is just short of luffing. Let it out until it shakes; then pull it back very slightly, simply to stop the shaking. In a perfectly trimmed boat the jib will start to luff slightly ahead of the mainsail.

It is often desirable to drop the jib just prior to working back through the anchorage. This is because the jib is one more device to trim while otherwise engaged, and also because jibs are located where they can obscure visibility ahead.

To "lie to" or use "automatic pilot" with a working jib set, simply cast off the jib sheets. In all other respects this maneuver remains the same as with mainsail alone.

Running with Jib and Mainsail

When running with jib and mainsail, the jib will be almost useless, since the wind will get to the larger mainsail first. Under these conditions, forget the jib entirely. If you wish to experiment, fasten a small pole or boat hook to the mast at one end, and engage the other end in the lower back jib corner. With this support, the jib can be held out to the windward side by using the windward sheet and thus be made to fill with air and help out. This is called sailing "wing and wing," and the pole is known as a "whisker pole."

Genoa jibs and spinnakers are exciting sails but should definitely be held up as projects for future learning. Only when fundamentals are mastered do these sails become easy and enjoyable to use.

chapter 14

The ABC's
of Sailing Safety

The aphorism "Experience is the best teacher because you get individual instruction" is true for sailing as well as for other matters. There is no substitute for "on-the-job training," i.e., hours spent sailing on the water. However, some important facets of sailing do not lend themselves to "on the job" study, and are best learned on bad weather days, at home in a comfortable chair.

Boat handling, though most important, is only one segment of the art of seamanship. This chapter will touch on several important seamanship skills related to boat handling: safety precautions, rules of the road, rescue techniques, anchoring, elementary navigation, manners afloat, and signals to the crew. Because a sailor must always prepare for the worst while doing his best to avoid it, insurance is also covered.

Twelve Rules for Safety Afloat

Obeying the following rules will minimize the possibility of mishaps.

1) Be sure the boat is properly equipped. Do not take equipment for granted!

2) Never go away from shore or dock without advising a responsible person of your plans. Let him know how long you plan to be out and where you plan to go.

3) Don't overload any craft—whether dinghy or sailboat.

4) Don't clown around in or with boats.

5) Learn and obey right-of-way rules.

6) Consult weather reports, and watch Coast Guard docks for small craft or other storm warnings. Keep an eye on the sky; it foretells all weather.

7) In small boats never cleat sheets. In calm weather you can get away with it, but calm weather habits carry over into heavy weather all too easily.

8) Take all precautions against falling overboard. If you don't swim, wear a life jacket at all times when afloat. Learn the man-overboard techniques described later in this chapter thoroughly.

9) Always stay with a capsized or swamped boat. These days, boats which can capsize are fitted with flotation gear, and they provide excellent protection. (If you buy an old boat, be sure you know the extent of its flotation capabilities.)

10) Know the waters in which you plan to sail. Consult charts, local sailors, fishermen, etc. Do not sail into waters with which you are unfamiliar.

11) Keep the boat under full control at all times. If you feel you are losing control, drop sails and anchor and think it through, or drop sails and tie to a convenient mooring.

12) Don't panic! Put the boat on "automatic pilot" and make a very serious effort to relax and drop your anxieties. This works!

Rules of the Road

As on land, marine traffic is controlled by right-of-way rules. Although these rules are quite basic and simple, they are one thing more that the newcomer to the sport must learn. He should study the rules carefully and memorize them. Again as on land, ignorance of the law is no excuse. On the water the law is written by the U.S. Coast Guard, and it is written pretty much as it is known throughout the world. The reference booklet is CG-169.

1) A vessel which is running free shall keep out of the way of a vessel which is closehauled.

2) A vessel which is closehauled on the port tack shall keep out of the way of a vessel which is closehauled on the starboard tack.

3) When both are running free, with the wind on different sides, the vessel which has the wind on the port side shall keep out of the way of the other.

4) When both are running free, with the wind on the same side, the vessel which is to the windward shall keep out of the way of the vessel which is to leeward.

5) A vessel which has the wind aft shall keep out of the way of the other vessel.

6) A vessel overtaking another vessel shall keep clear of the overtaken vessel.

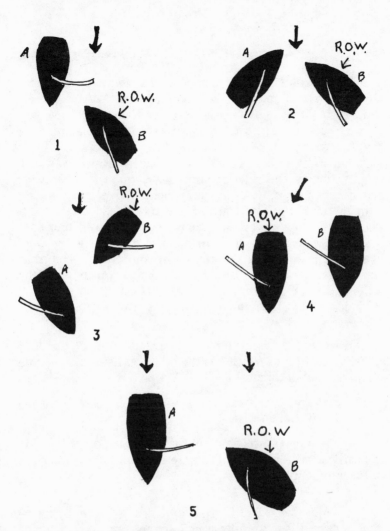

Figure 14-1. Rules of the road.
1. Both boats have wind on same side, but B has right-of-way because it is sailing as close as possible to wind. 2. Whenever two boats are sailing with sails on opposite sides, the one with the sail on the left (wind from right side) has right-of-way. 3. Both boats have the wind from behind but their sails on different sides. Because A has its sail on the right side, it must keep out of the way of B. 4. Both boats have the wind behind and on the same side. A has right-of-way because B has its sails toward A. 5. Both boats have wind on same side, but B has right-of-way because it is sailing closer to the wind. Note that this caption material "translates" the CG wording.

In most cases powerboats must give way to sailboats. However, a boat under sail *and* power is considered a power-boat just as if its sails were lowered. About the only way to identify such a boat is to look for exhaust vapors from the engine.

A large power boat cannot be expected to give way to a small sailboat. The rules require that a small sailboat *must* give way to a large, unwieldy powerboat.

In the early days of learning the sport, many sailors un-wisely tend to give everyone else the right-of-way rather than risk being wrong. However, when a boat has the right of way, its skipper is obligated to maintain its course and speed so as not to "balk," or confuse, the other boat which is in the act of steering clear.

Under power alone, the following basic rules apply:

1) When two vessels are crossing so as to involve risk of collision, the vessel which has the other on its own right side shall keep out of the way.

2) Every vessel overtaking another shall keep out of the way of the overtaken vessel.

3) When two vessels are approaching each other head on or nearly so with risk of collision, each shall turn to the right sufficiently to avoid risk.

The sailor can identify risk of collision, when circumstances permit, by carefully watching the compass bearing of an approaching vessel. *If that bearing does not appreciably change, risk of collision should be deemed to exist.*

Those without a compass can determine risk of collision as follows: the sailor simply lines up the boat in question with a fixed object on his own boat, carefully maintaining his point of observation (any movement by the sailor will naturally af-

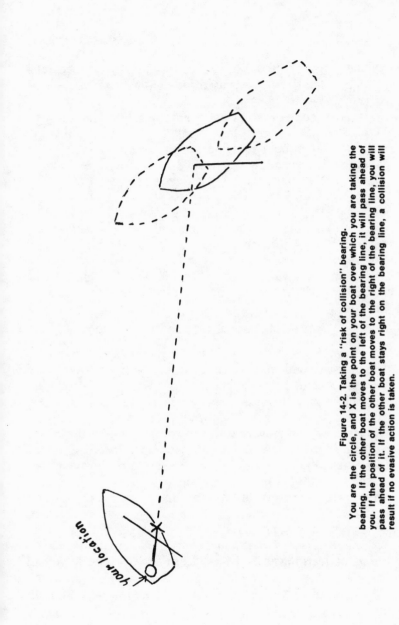

Figure 14-2. Taking a "risk of collision" bearing.

You are the circle, and X is the point on your boat over which you are taking the bearing. If the other boat moves to the left of the bearing line, it will pass ahead of you. If the position of the other boat moves to the right of the bearing line, you will pass ahead of it. If the other boat stays right on the bearing line, a collision will result if no evasive action is taken.

fect the bearing). If the other boat remains in a fixed relationship to the fixed object used for sighting, risk of collision
exists.

If risk of collision does exist, appropriate action must be
taken as quickly as possible, not only to avoid collision but to
signal the other boat that the action is being taken. When
avoiding another boat which has the right-of-way, *never* cross
in front of the other boat.

The General Prudential Rule for Sailors states that in
obeying and construing the rules of the road, due regard shall
be had to all dangers of navigation and collision, and to any
special circumstances which may render a departure from all
the above rules necessary in order to avoid immediate
danger. In other words, no matter who has the right-of-way
by the basic rules, every sailor must use judgment and avoid
collision.

Man-Overboard Rescue Procedure

It goes without saying that small children and other nonswimmers should not be out sailing with inexperienced
skippers. Accidents do happen on the water, mostly due to
insufficient preparedness, poor judgment, or ignorance. One
accident that should never happen is a drowning.

Persons who can swim well should have no fear of falling
overboard, providing the skipper is experienced in rescue
techniques. Passengers of any age who do not swim well
should wear life vests at all times on any boat.

For both swimmers and nonswimmers, the temperature of
the water is an important factor in survival. In warm water
one can tread water for hours with no real discomfort, but in
cold water resistance is low and energy quick to diminish.

Part of learning to sail is to learn safety measures of all
kinds. The skipper cannot be expected to teach his guests the
techniques of rescuing, but he should know them himself.

Note: It must again be emphasized that in this book we deal *only* with light airs,
small boats and neglible wave height. For other conditions, differing and/or additional rescue techniques might be needed.

Rescuing someone in the water, whether he is conscious or not, is not difficult, particularly from small boats with decks an easy arm's reach above water level. However, rescue techniques require understanding of the basic maneuvers and sufficient practice to commit these maneuvers to reflex. When a rescue operation is required, speed is almost invariably needed.

At the call "man overboard!", take the following steps:

1) Throw over a life jacket or other floating object as quickly as possible to enable the swimmer to reach and use it.

2) Turn so as to steer for the swimmer and arrive close to him under control but at minimum speed.

3) Grab swimmer firmly and pull him aboard; or, if he is unconscious, pass a line around him, tie a knot in it, and pull him aboard. (Under these conditions, adrenalin makes incredible amounts of strength available!)

4) After working the water out of the victim's lungs, administer mouth-to-mouth resuscitation, if necessary. (Keep a first aid book aboard!)

Rescue maneuvers can be started while sailing close-hauled, reaching, or running. Although the technical details differ, from all three courses the basic procedure is the same: Jibe, steer for a point in the water one or more boat lengths (depending on wave and wind strength) downwind from the swimmer, and turn directly toward the swimmer just *before* reaching that downwind point. A slight angle of the boat to the wind is advisable to make it possible to stretch the momentum distance by pulling the sheet in, and to prevent the boat's striking the swimmer. One can see a small object in the water (swimmers' heads *are* small) better over the side than over the bow of the boat. Make very sure the approach to the swimmer is not upwind of him; if it is, the boat will be driven downwind much more rapidly than will the low-profile head of the swimmer, and the vessel may run into him.

From sailing close-hauled, turn quickly to a beam reach—beam, not close or broad—freeing the sheet to suit the change in course. If a working jib is in use, releasing and forgetting it will avoid complications. During this beam reach the boat is, of course, sailing *away from* the swimmer. It is necessary to get a few boat lengths away from him in order to gain maneuvering space. Next make the turn back to the swimmer by jibe, not by tacking; tacking places the boat farther upwind, whereas its desired location (after turning 180 degrees) is downwind of the swimmer. Sail back toward that imaginary point downwind of, and slightly toward you from, the swimmer. Make a normal turn toward the swimmer's downwind side.

From a beam reach, continue on the reach until distance from the swimmer allows you to turn and make all other moves as above. From a broad reach, quickly change the course to a beam reach, with attendant sheet adjustment. Thereafter, all moves are the same as above. From a close reach, change the course to a beam reach, but ease out the sheet to suit.

From a run, the procedure is the same as from a broad reach except that the turn is longer and the sheet comes in from a farther out position to attain the needed beam reach. Then, because the swimmer is upwind of you, *tack* instead of jibing (see Figure 14-6).

It goes without saying that the "Man overboard!" call is never anticipated. For this reason, it is very important to practice the steps until they become committed to reflex action.

Anchoring

There are times when circumstances require anchoring—for instance, when the wind drops to a calm and tidal currents

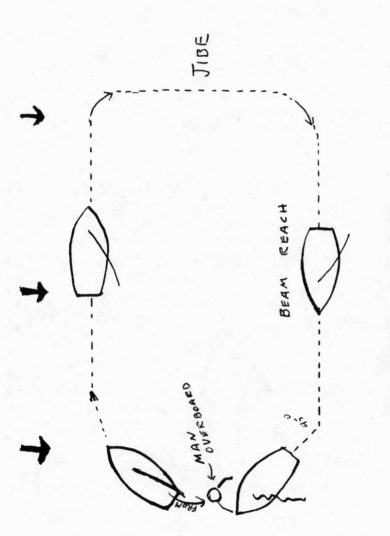

Figure 14-3. Rescuing man overboard from a beat.
Assume a beam reach, jibe, and return to swimmer at a 45-degree angle and toward his downwind side.

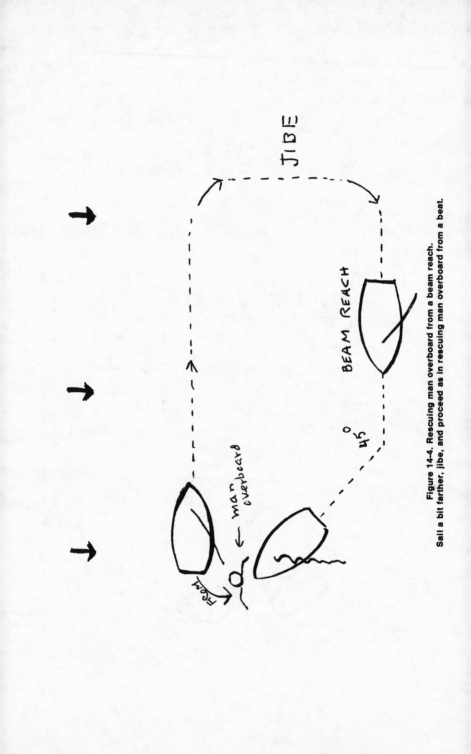

Figure 14-4. Rescuing man overboard from a beam reach.
Sail a bit farther, jibe, and proceed as in rescuing man overboard from a beat.

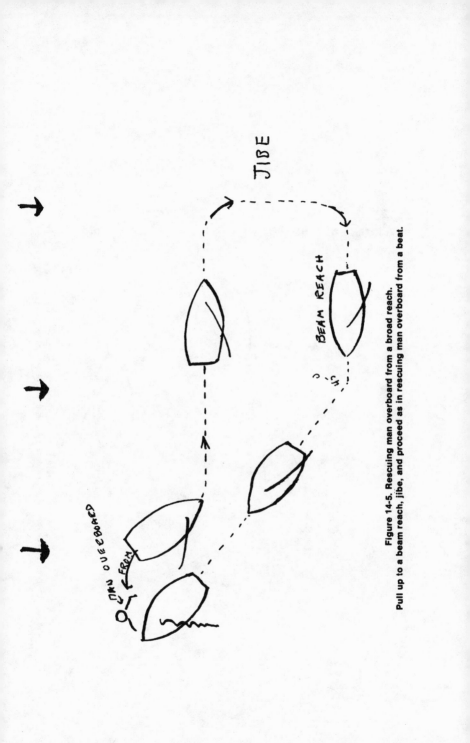

Figure 14-5. Rescuing man overboard from a broad reach.
Pull up to a beam reach, jibe, and proceed as in rescuing man overboard from a beat.

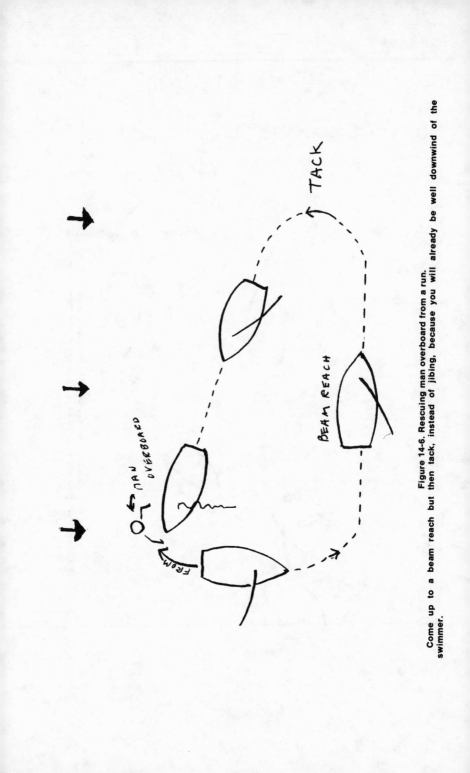

Figure 14-6. Rescuing man overboard from a run. Come up to a beam reach but then tack, instead of jibing, because you will already be well downwind of the swimmer.

cause a drift toward an obstruction or when a sudden wind squall makes it unwise to continue sailing. In keeping with the intent to discuss sailing, not motorboating, this topic skirts the rather obvious use of an engine under these circumstances.

Of course, not all circumstances for anchoring are unpleasant ones. More often the anchor will be used in a quiet cove during meals, social get-togethers and so on.

Excepting emergencies, the newcomer to sailing will do his anchoring in waters 25 feet deep or less. Minimal equipment for such waters would be one anchor and 125 feet of good anchor line. A very cautious sailor who might expect to sail offshore occasionally would have two anchors and at least 300 feet of line for each.

Several types of anchor are available, each with its peculiar advantages. The Danforth is usually well suited to small boat use, being light as well as efficient in holding power. However, a length of heavy chain attached to the Danforth will allow it to dig in better; its light weight otherwise tends to make it skitter across the bottom.

Anchoring with a Danforth simply requires throwing it overboard. There is no wrong way to do it, as there is with some designs which can foul their lines if not carefully lowered. However, be certain that the other end of the anchor line is fastened to the boat. Elementary? It is a fact that many expensive anchors lie on the bottom because of neglect in this matter.

The length of line to let out in anchoring depends upon water depth and height of deck above water level. The ratio of line length to water depth is called "scope," and a recommended scope for short-term, good-weather anchoring is five to one *from water level*. If the waves are running high, with attendant hard jerking at the anchor line, let the scope out to six or seven to one. If the boat is to be left untended for some time in high waves, make the scope up to ten to one.

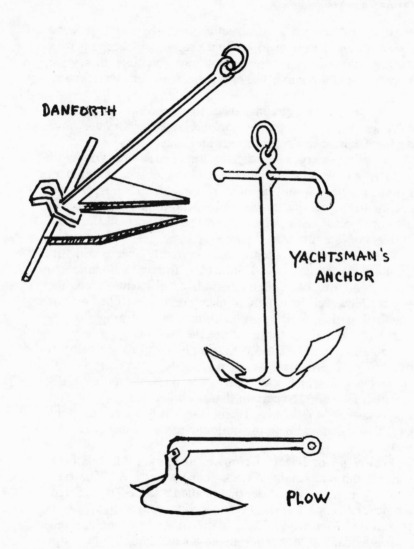

DANFORTH

YACHTSMAN'S ANCHOR

PLOW

Figure 14-7. Anchors.

Once the anchor is dropped and the wind or current has brought the boat to the end of the scope so that the anchor line is taut from deck to bottom, one must observe carefully whether the boat is still drifting or is being firmly held by the anchor. To make this observation, select two fixed objects on shore, as far distant from each other and as nearly in line with each other and with the boat as possible. These two objects form a range, and any movement of the boat will be clearly observable in the movement of these range objects toward or away from each other. If their alignment changes, the boat is moving; if there is no alignment change, the anchor is holding. Of course, the boat will swing some at anchor because of wind shifts, but such swinging will be on a short arc as long as the anchor is holding. It is simple to identify this swinging and not confuse it with drifting. If there is drifting, jerking hard on the anchor line will sometimes set the anchor flukes into the bottom. Letting out more scope might do the job (the more acute the angle of the line, the better the flukes can engage). All else failing, pull the anchor back on deck and restart the process. Sometimes moving just a few yards from a poor anchoring spot will bring success. Rocky or weedy patches on the bottom, the most common causes for anchor failure, are usually marked on the chart of local waters. In areas where the bottom is generally rocky or weedy, heavier anchors are better. This is one of the reasons why cruising sailors have more than one anchor aboard.

Elementary Navigation and Chart-reading

The word "navigation" covers many related fields—celestial, coastwise, dead reckoning, and piloting—but in essence it merely means plotting the course for a boat; getting across the harbor is navigation as much as is crossing the Atlantic. The topic can be a fascinating one, involving aspects of astronomy, physics, hydrology, trigonometry, aerology, and other subjects. A few simple rudiments will serve as a starter.

As a reference for the study of navigation, or of many other nautical fields, the purchase of Chapman's *Piloting, Seamanship and Small Boat Handling* or an equivalent book is highly recommended. The sailor should also acquire a chart of the local waters. Both items are readily available at most supply stores.

Driving to a waterside location affording an overlook of the local sailing area, the sailor can spread the chart out in orientation with his location. The chart includes the main docks and wharves in their relationship to other salients, such as points of land and shoals. It shows church steeples, as well as unique structures of other types, and indicates all government buoys. Water depths are noted on the chart throughout all water areas, and topological contours are drawn in. In short, a nautical chart is an excellent device for aid in navigation. Because of space limitations, many symbols are used. Every chart explains some of these, but all are explained in Chart number 1, U.S.A., *Nautical Chart Symbols and Abbreviations,* which is a useful adjunct to purchase along with the local chart.

Harbor and River Buoys

The three R's of piloting—Red, Right, Return—constitute one of the fundamental rules of navigation in harbors, rivers, bays, and intracoastal waterways. The rule means that when a sailor is "returning," i.e., navigating into port or up a river, he will find red government buoys on the right side of the channel. The chart shows these red buoys as red diamonds. Some of these markers, in the shape of truncated cones and called nuns, are simple buoys without light or sound. They are designated on the chart by the letter "N" in conjunction with even numbers; for example, N 2, N 4, N

6, etc. If a light is mounted on a marker, its color and characteristic are specified on the chart; "fl R 4 sec" means "red light flashing every four seconds." Righthand buoys may have red or white lights. If the buoy is a bell or a gong, these facts are written out; if it has both light and gong, both are noted. Buoys may have any of a number of light characteristics—flashing, fixed, occulting, quick-flashing, and others. Chart number 1 is the best text for the study of this subject.

The left side of a channel has black markers. Simple ones, cylindrical in shape, are called cans. Others may have lights, bells, or gongs, and their light characteristics may vary. Colors of lights on the "black side" are restricted to white and green. Simple black buoys have odd numbers, and number 1 is always at the entrance to the harbor or river. These buoys are designated on the chart as C 1, C 3, C 5, etc. Black buoys with gongs are labeled "gong," black buoys with fixed white lights are labeled "FW," and so on.

Although some waterways have shapes other than those of nun and can, and sometimes other colors may be used in conjunction with black or red, the three R's are basic to all navigation in coastal waters.

An apocryphal yarn is told about the admiral whose public appearance in triumphant retirement was the occasion for many eulogies about his vaunted navigation feats. When asked for his secret, he simply raised his sleeve to reveal the tattooed inscription: "Red, Right, Return."

Manners Afloat

"Good manners" on the water means the same things that it means on land: getting along well with people under varying circumstances, thoughtfulness, courtesy, and kindness. To cite some examples, it is good nautical manners to:

1) Refrain from throwing anything, even a cigarette stub, overboard anywhere. It is later than we think, and failure to observe antipollution common sense will increasingly impinge on the rights of all other people.

2) Go to the assistance of other vessels in any kind of distress, providing that in doing so the good Samaritan does not unreasonably endanger his own life or property.

3) Keep well away from the windward side of other boats sailing, even when you are under power and with sails down. Any sizable object to windward of a boat under sail interferes with that vessel's sailing efficiency and can even cause lack of control.

4) Use as little time and space as possible when "parking" at a busy dock or float to take on ice, supplies, or fuel.

5) Refrain from sailing through a racing fleet in action, if at all possible. If the sailor must do so, he should try very hard to favor the downwind side. Inches are important to a racer, and interference with a competitor's wind can make a difference of one or more places in the fleet.

6) Refrain from pressing the right-of-way, if doing so would seriously discommode another sailor.

7) Call attention of one's skipper to obstacles ahead which he may not be able to see. In a sailboat this is not "back seat driving," and is considered very helpful.

Signals to the Crew

Whether knowledgeable or otherwise, guests aboard will appreciate being told in advance about any contemplated activities, such as changes in course, tacking, jibes, etc. Guests enjoy being let in on the sailing plan. Before the sailor leaves the dock, he should let each guest know which responsibilities of boat handling, if any, he is to assume. It is also useful to tell the tyros in the group what each of the various lines is for, and to explain how idle tinkering can cause problems.

Perhaps the most often used communications to others aboard are signals to warn them of the imminent swinging of the boom in tacking or jibing. In small boats the boom is low enough to be a menace when someone is standing, or even sitting upright, and few novices expect decapitation.

The time-honored signals employed by sailors are:

1) "Prepare to come about," or "Ready about." This alerts the crew to the plan. The skipper refrains from further action until the crew has made pertinent preparations and so signaled.

2) "Helm's a-lee," or "Hard a-lee," when the tiller is started into the turn. The first phrase, incidentally, is a complete outline to the novice skipper of what he must do. Putting the helm (tiller) to the lee side makes the boat come about. Lee side is sail side.

Signals for jibing are:

1) "Prepare to jibe."
2) "Jibe ho."
3) "Helm's a-weather."

In giving instructions to novices aboard, try to forget new-found nautical words. One's sailing ability will advertise his expertise far more intelligibly than jargon can.

Insurance

Following the procedures and precautions outlined previously in this chapter will minimize the possibility of accidents. Nevertheless, a sailor would be foolhardy not to carry insurance.

Information on insurance may be acquired from yacht brokers and insurance brokers. Any marina operator will be of help in this area also.

There are basically two kinds of insurance which concern the yacht owner: Hull and P and I (Protection and Indemnity).

Hull insurance may be bought in either of two coverages, Named Peril and All Risk. The perils named in the former are sinking, stranding, burning, collision, and heavy weather; and protection is limited to those hazards. All Risk policies cover all the named perils in addition to such broad areas as "latent defects" and "carelessness." These items are analogous to the "mysterious disappearance" coverage available for home owners' policies. Needless to say, the All Risk marine policy is the more popular despite its higher cost.

All Risk policies cover liability for property damage and personal injury, but only up to the total of the boat's insured value. For this reason most responsible owners add a P and I policy for their peace of mind, although such is not legally requisite on the water. P and I is available in any desired amount, within reason.

The standard policies named above also include racing coverage, except for loss of or damage to spinnakers, which usually requires separate coverage.

Welcome to the Sailing Fraternity

People who are bitten by the sailing bug never get over it—and why should they? Sailing satisfies the atavistic human desire to match wits and skill against the unpredictability of the elements. And the elements are unpredictable indeed on the water. Sometimes the wind whistles and then, suddenly, it will die away entirely. Every summer has glorious sailing days in which sunlight sparkles on blue water affectionately ruffled by a fine sailing breeze; but if all the days were like that, sailors wouldn't so vividly remember their wonder and beauty. That is why sailors actually welcome the rain, the squalls, and the salt spray encrusting their glasses. So, you see, in sailing there is no such thing as bad weather; there are only different kinds of good weather.

Sailing is one of the best ways there is of getting back to nature. Meeting the challenges of their sport helps sailors to realize the importance of cooperation with their fellow navigators. That is why sailors are so ready and glad to help a skipper in trouble.

So welcome to the sailing fraternity! You will find it a true brotherhood of wonderful people the world over who enjoy one of the most challenging, exciting, and yet serenely satisfying sports known to man.

Glossary

ABAFT. Toward the stern.

ABEAM. The direction at right angles to the boat's centerline.

AFT. At, toward, or near the stern.

AMIDSHIPS. The area of any vessel midway between bow and stern and between the sides.

BACKSTAYS. Lengths of wire rope leading from the mast to the deck, to secure the mast from bending forward. Called running backstays if adjustable, and permanent backstays if not adjustable.

BALLAST. Weight concentrated at the lowest point in a boat to aid in stabilization by lowering the center of gravity. Weight (lead or iron) in keels is called "outside ballast," while movable weights (lead, iron, etc.) inside the boat are "inside ballast."

BATTEN POCKETS. Pockets which hold the battens in the sail.

BATTENS. Thin wooden or plastic strips used to stiffen the roach in the leach of a sail.

BEAM. The width of a boat.

BEAR OFF. To turn away from the wind, i.e., downwind.

BEAT. As a verb, to sail to windward. As a noun, windward course, as in sailing "on a beat."

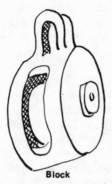

Block

BEND. To make a sail fast to a spar or stay by means of knots, hooks, slide/track, or groove. Also, to secure with a bend (knot or tie).

BIGHT. A curve in a line before it becomes a loop. Also, a curve in the shoreline.

BILGE. The turn of the hull below the waterline; also, the area inside the hull where water collects above and near the keelson.

BITT. A post with a pin through it for fastening rope.

BITTER END. The free end of a rope fastened to a device on a boat.

BLOCK. Nautical word for pulley. It may have one or more wheels, called "sheaves."

BOLT ROPE. The rope sewn into the edge of a sail, usually along the luff.

BOOM. A spar at the bottom of a sail. Also, the pole used to hold spinnakers out from boat.

BOW (pronounced "bough"). The front end of a boat.

BRIDLE. A length of wire of which both ends are fastened and to which a pulling force is applied at a point within its length. In small sail-

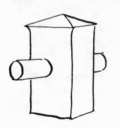

Bitt

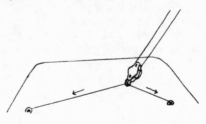

Bridle

boats a bridle is almost always used near the stern of the boat, running from near one side to near the other. On it is a block, part of the mainsheet; the bridle allows this block to travel across the boat when one changes tacks. Sail efficiency is thereby increased.

BROACH. To swing sharply toward wind when running, because of heavy seas, poor steering, or poor rudder design.

BUMPERS. Soft, tough devices used to protect the sides of boats from docks, piles, other boats, etc.

BURDENED VESSEL. That craft required to keep clear of the craft holding right-of-way (cf. Privileged vessel).

CENTERBOARD. A movable, stiff device pivoted to drop down or be pulled up, located on the boat's centerline for the purpose of securing against sideward slip and also to enable the craft to be navigated in water too shallow for boats with permanent lateral plane (keel). When raised, the centerboard is housed in waterproof sheath (centerboard box or trunk).

CENTERLINE. The front-to-back center of a boat.

CHAIN PLATES. Metal plates bolted to the side of a boat to receive shrouds and stays.

CHARTS. Nautical maps containing aids to navigation, water depths, shoals, landmarks, and terrain topography.

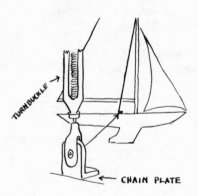

Chain Plate   **Chock**

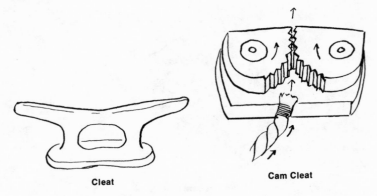

Cleat   Cam Cleat

CHOCK. A metal or plastic casting through which lines are led to shore
    or other vessels and which guides these lines to avoid chafing.

CLEAT. A device made of plastic, wood, or metal to hold a line secure.
    The standard cleat has two horns around which the line is tied for
    maximum friction. A cam cleat has two moving, spring-loaded
    cams which grab the line securely to keep it from running in one
    direction, but by spreading apart allow it to run easily in the other
    direction. A jam cleat is similar to a cam cleat, except that the line
    is jammed down between two toothed friction parts to secure it,
    then jerked away from these parts for freeing.

CLEW. The lower aft corner of a Marconi (triangular) sail.

CLOSE-HAULED. Sailing as close as possible to the wind, with sails
    trimmed for beating (close to the boat's centerline). Also known as
    "on the wind," "beating," and "strapped down."

COAMING. A raised protection around the cockpit.

COCKPIT. The area of a boat allocated to the crew for sailing and sitting.
    An open cockpit has no drains (scuppers) to eliminate rain or
    spray. A self-bailing cockpit has scuppers and hence does not need
    pumping.

CRINGLE. An eye of metal (grommet) worked into a sail with thread or
    light line for securing purposes.

CUDDY. A decked shelter, less commodious than a cabin.

DAGGER BOARD. A movable stiff member used to avoid side slip, pushed
    down or lifted up vertically from a sheath (house or trunk).

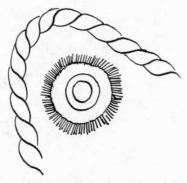

Cringle in Corner of Sail

DECK PLATE. A plate bolted to the deck. Usually made with an eye to accept shackles or blocks. Sometimes called a "pad eye."

DOWNHAUL. A rope or rope/block combination used to pull down the boom to tighten the luff of the mainsail, and other sails.

DRAFT. The distance from a vessel's waterline to the bottom of its hull, keel, or board.

EASE. To relieve pressure on sail or helm by letting the sheet out, "easing her up" toward the wind, etc.

EYE SPLICE. A splice making the end of a rope into a loop.

FAIRLEAD. A simple eye or smooth casting designed to guide a line where tension does not require a block. It may be adjustable on a track.

FETCH. To reach an objective without coming about, e.g., "He can fetch the buoy on the starboard tack." As a noun, the distance wind or

Fairleads
Left: Cast. *Right:* Bull's-eye.

tide has, free of obstruction, e.g., "The wind has a fetch of ten miles."

FLY. A masthead pennant, pointer, or windsock to indicate the apparent wind. Also a ribbon or piece of yarn in the rigging for the same purpose.

FOOT. Lower edge of a sail. As a verb, to make good time, usually on a beat. ("Footing" and "pointing" refer to the speed and the angle of boat to wind, respectively.)

FORWARD. To the front, e.g., "The anchorline is forward of the mast," or "The dock is still forward of us."

FREE. Sailing with the wind anywhere from abeam to directly behind; e.g., running and sailing on a beam or broad reach are "sailing free." As verb, to cast off, to release, to untangle, etc.

FREEBOARD. Vertical distance from waterline to deck.

FURL. To wrap a sail neatly to a spar.

GENOA JIB. Large, overlapping jib.

GOOSENECK. A metal fitting designed like a universal joint which secures boom to mast.

HALYARD. Fiber or wire line used to raise sails.

Gooseneck

HARD A-LEE. Short for "The helm is hard a-lee," the signal signifying the movement of the rudder incident to turning.

HEAD. Upper corner of a Marconi sail. Also a boat's toilet.

HEADBOARD. The stiffener, of wood or plastic, fitted into the head of a sail.

HEADREACHING. Carrying momentum, or way, while sailing into the wind.

HEADSTAY. The stay running from mast to stem area, to secure mast from bending backward.

HEAD TO WIND. Headed into wind, with sails shaking.

HEADWAY. Forward motion.

HEAVE. To throw or cast. Also, to pull on a rope. As noun, the rise and fall of a vessel in a seaway.

HEEL. To tip, tilt, lay over. As noun, the amount of tilting, expressed in degrees.

HELM. The lever used to move a rudder. Also, the tendency of a vessel to steer relative to the wind if left to its own devices; e.g., "weather helm" means tending to steer toward the wind.

HULL. The main body of a boat as distinct from spars, rigging, centerboard, etc.

IN IRONS (IN STAYS). A condition in which a boat faces the wind and has lost all headway.

JIB. A triangular sail used in front of the mast.

JIBE (GYBE). To change tacks by turning away from the wind, toward the sail.

JIB-HEADED. Synonymous with Marconi or Bermudian, to describe triangular sails. Like a jib.

JIBSTAY. Stay on which a jib is hanked (hooked) to be raised.

JUMPER STRUT. A single or forked strut on the front side of a mast to increase stability of upper part of mast, coupled with jumper stays.

KEEL. Backbone of a boat's structure. Also, the fixed protuberance designed to counteract leeway (sideslip).

KEELSON (pronounced "kelson"). A timber or metal stringer located over the keel as a strengthening member.

KNOT. Any of a myriad of friction devices designed to restrain line from slipping. Also, a measure of rate of speed. One knot means "one nautical mile per hour." A nautical mile is equivalent to one minute of latitude or longitude, and is 1.15 statute miles.

LANYARD. A short piece of light line used for all manner of temporary ties.

LATERAL PLANE. The area of a boat designed to offset drift or slippage. It includes the hull and keel or centerboard.

LAY. Of a rope, the direction of twist of the component yarns or fibers. As a verb, to fetch.

LAYLINE. The line on which a boat can fetch a mark or buoy.

LEACH. The aft edge of a sail.

LEE. Opposite to windward. A lee shore is that shore at which the wind blows. The lee side of anything is the side away from the wind. "Leeward" means "toward the lee side." "A-lee" is short for "to leeward." "By the lee" means running with the wind slightly off to the side of the sail (as compared with normal location of the wind on side opposite the sail).

LEEWAY. Distance slipped to leeward. No boat is 100 percent efficient in maintaining a steered course.

LIGHT SAILS. Sails, such as spinnakers, made of lightweight cloth.

LINES. Shipboard terminology for "ropes." Also, the drawings by which a hull's shape is depicted.

LIST. Leaning of a vessel due to heavier weight on one side.

LUFF. The forward edge of a sail. As a verb, to shake, applied to a sail when its head is to the wind; also, to cause the sail to shake. E.g., "The sail is luffing," and "to luff the boat into the wind."

MAINMAST. The sole mast of a catboat or sloop; the principal mast of larger boats.

MAINSAIL. The sail rigged on the afterside of the mainmast.

MAINSHEET. Control line used on mainsail.

MAKE FAST. To tie up, secure.

MARCONI. Fore-and-aft or triangular (jib-headed) sail. This sail shape became popular about the time that Guglielmo Marconi put up his first tall transmitting mast and attendant stays.

MAST. A vertical spar on which sails are hoisted.

MOOR. To secure to a mooring.

MOORING. The relatively permanent arrangement by which a vessel is secured while not sailing. As in anchoring, a moored boat is free to move in a complete circle with wind shifts.

OFFSHORE. Away from a shore, e.g., "The large boat is farther offshore than the small one," or "Today we have an offshore breeze."

OFF THE WIND. Sailing on any course other than close-hauled.

ON THE WIND. Close-hauled.

OUTBOARD. Beyond the hull.

OUTHAUL. A line used to secure and adjust the clew of a sail.

OVERSTAND. To go unnecessarily beyond the "layline," q.v.

PAINTER. A piece of line, attached to the boat's bow, for securing a boat to another object.

PART. To break. As noun, the "standing part" (main part) of a line, also called "hauling part" or "running part."

PAY OFF, PAY OUT. To slacken, to ease out a length of line. Of a boat, to turn away from the wind with the bow.

PENDANT. A short piece of line, usually wire, used to secure any of a number of devices. One such is the pendant used to hold up a boat's boom when the boat is not in use.

PENNANT. (1) The length of fiber or wire line by which a boat is fastened to its mooring. (2) A long, narrow, usually triangular flag. (3) Pendant.

PINCH. To sail a boat inefficiently close to the wind.

POINT. To head high, close to the wind.

PORT. Left.

PORT TACK. Sailing course with the wind from the port side.

PRIVILEGED VESSEL. Vessel with right-of-way.

QUARTER. That part of a boat's side which lies between the beam and the stern.

RAIL. Outer edge of the deck.

RAKE. Inclination of a mast from the vertical, fore and aft.

REACH. Any sailing course between close-hauled and running. As verb, to sail on a reach. (See Chapter 8.)

READY ABOUT! Spoken signal to alert crew that tacking is imminent.

REEVE. To pass a line through a block or fairlead.

RIDE. To lie at anchor. Also, to "ride out" a storm.

RIG. The character of a boat's sail plan and mast arrangement.

RIGGING. The entire complex of spars, sails, lines, and blocks. Standing rigging is relatively permanent, while running rigging includes the components which move in the working of the vessel.

ROACH. The curve in the foot, leach, or luff of a sail.

RODE. Anchor line.

RUN. To sail almost directly before the wind. Also, the aft underwater shape of a hull.

SAIL STOPS. Straps made of sailcloth, or lengths of rope or shock cord, used to tie a sail to a spar or other device.

SEAWAY. An area in which seas are running.

SECURE. To fasten, make fast.

SHACKLE. Any of a variety of U-shaped metal fittings with a pin or screw across the open end used to join two objects.

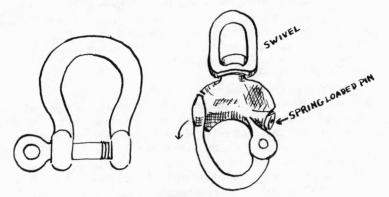

Shackles
Left: Plain. *Right:* Snap.

SHEAVE (pronounced "shiv"). The wheel in a pulley, or block.

SHEER. The curve of a vessel's deck from bow to stern. As a verb, "to sheer off" means "to bear away, to avoid contact."

SHEET. Any rope used to control a sail, e.g., mainsheet, jib sheet, etc.

SHROUDS. Side stays supporting masts.

SKEG. A stiff member located ahead of a rudder separated from the keel or centerboard area. Also, in power boats a member extending below the propeller for protection.

SKIPPER. Person in command. Helmsman.

SLIP. A mooring or docking area between two small piers or floating booms.

SNAP HOOKS. Hooks with spring-loaded closure.

SOLE. The floor of a boat's cockpit or cabin.

SPAR. Term covering all wooden stiffeners, such as mast, boom, gaff, spinnaker pole, etc.

SPINNAKER. Lightweight sail of great area, used when boat is reaching or running.

SPREADER. Strut, usually horizontal and lateral, used to spread rigging for strength in offsetting tendency of mast to bend with the wind pressure.

STARBOARD. Right.

STARBOARD TACK. Sailing course with the wind from the starboard side.

STAYS. Lengths of wire rope used to support mast, fore and aft. Stays include the headstay, jib stay, forestay, and backstay.

STEM. The foremost timber in a boat, made of wood, plastic, or metal.

STERN. The aftermost extremity of a boat.

STERNWAY. Backward motion.

STOPS. Straps to secure sail to boom in a furl.

TACK. The forward lower corner of a sail. Also, a straight course. As a verb, to change from one tack to another while coming about. One changes tacks when either jibing or coming about. In jibing, the boat is often said to be changing from one "jibe" to another.

TENDER. Lacking resistance to heeling, or lacking stiffness. Opposite is "stiff." Also, a dinghylike craft which may be sailed, powered, or rowed, and used to transport personnel and supplies between boat and shore.

THIMBLE. A round or pear-shaped device grooved to take a rope in an eye splice; it is used for fastening other devices to that rope.

THWARTSHIPS. Across the boat.

TILLER. A wooden lever, or bar, used to move the rudder, and hence steer the boat.

TOPSIDES. The sides of a boat above the waterline.

TRANSOM. Loosely, stern. More specifically, a broad, nearly vertical stern.

TRAVELER. A track located near the back end of a sailboat, running from near one side of the boat to near the other side. On it rides a slide to which is fastened a block, part of the mainsheet. The traveler enables the sheet to move from one side to the other when the boat is tacked. Sail efficiency is thereby increased.

TRIM. To adjust a sail in relation to wind direction and boat course. Also, the balance of a boat, either fore and aft or thwartships.

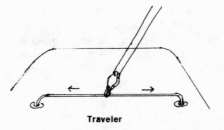

Traveler

TURNBUCKLE. A threaded link which pulls two devices together. Used in stays and shrouds for adjusting tension.

VEER. Of the wind, to shift in a clockwise direction. The verb "haul," when applied to the wind, also means to shift in a clockwise direction. When the wind shifts counterclockwise, it "backs."

WAKE. Waves, or otherwise disturbed water, caused by the drag or resistance of a vessel when it passes through the water.

WATERLINE. Dividing line between topsides and underbody of a boat.

WAY. Movement through the water; cf. Headway, Sternway. A moving boat is said to be underway.

WELL FOUND. Well equipped, with all components in good condition.

WHISKER POLE. Light pole or stick used to hold out a working jib to windward so as to allow it to fill with wind.

WINCH. Small, drum-shaped device, used to increase mechanical advantage for pulling in a line against considerable tension. Line is wound clockwise, three or more turns.

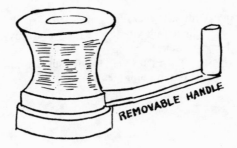

Winch

WINDWARD. Toward the wind. Synonym, "weather." Opposite of leeward. E.g., "the windward (weather) side."

WING AND WING. Describing the use of mainsail and working jib in which the jib is "wung-out" on the side opposite the mainsail to increase sail area when running or broad reaching.

Wing and Wing

WORKING SAILS. Ordinary, everyday sails, such as small jib and mainsail, exclusive of light sails or storm sails (very heavy, small sails for use in heavy weather).

YACHT. Any vessel used exclusively for pleasure, from a rowboat to the largest private ocean-going steamer.

Index

(*Note:* Page numbers in italics refer to illustrations.)